Pet Food Nation

D0169612

Pet Food Nation

The SMART, EASY, and HEALTHY
Way to Feed Your Pet Now

Joan Weiskopf

Collins
An Imprint of HarperCollinsPublishers

This book is written as a source of information only. The information contained in this book should by no means be considered a substitute for the advice of a qualified veterinary professional, who should always be consulted before beginning any new food regime for your pet.

All efforts have been made to ensure the accuracy of the information contained in this book as of the date published. The author and the publisher expressly disclaim responsibility for any adverse effects arising from the use or application of the information contained herein.

HarperCollins books may be purchased for educational, business, or sales promotional use. For information, please write: Special Markets Department, Harper-Collins Publishers, 10 East 53rd Street, New York, NY 10022.

FIRST EDITION

Designed by Lorie Pagnozzi

Library of Congress Cataloging-in-Publication Data has been applied for.

ISBN 978-0-06-145500-1
ISBN-10 0-06-145500-8

07 08 09 10 11 DIX/RRD 10 9 8 7 6 5 4 3 2 1

Ruth and Donny, Elaine, Lenora, Sue

Five angels who believe

"The greatness of a nation and its moral progress can be judged

by the way its animals are treated."

—Mahatma Gandhi

Acknowledgments

The kind man feeds his beast before sitting down to dinner.——Hebrew Proverb

Nature does not call for long recipes.——Paracelsus

This has been quite a journey, with the genuine spirit of HarperCollins illuminating the way. Maureen O'Brien, Lisa Sharkey, and Stephanie Fraser, you are the best.

Marcia and Julia, thanks for getting me started.

Michael Coffey, my writing angel, has proved that a great listener can tell a great story.

Contents

Part Three: Home Cooking Recipes

Note to the Reader: A Call to Action

Early in 2007, in response to customer complaints that their pets were getting sick from bad food, a Canadian pet food manufacturer, Menu Foods, ran a controlled test. Twenty-five cats and fifteen dogs were given the Menu product; in short order, nine cats and one dog died. This prompted a call to the U.S. Food and Drug Administration in mid-March and the immediate recall of sixty million cans and pouches of dog and cat food that had originated at the Toronto plant. Suspicion centered on wheat gluten, a protein source and binder found in many pet foods. Menu had only recently changed suppliers for the gluten, and it was believed that the new supplier, based in China, had provided gluten contami-

nated with melamine, a chemical used in making plastic cut-
lery and also used in fertilizer.

It was not only the poor animals involved in the controlled test that were affected.

Q. In light of the pet food recall, should I
stop feeding my dog commercial pet food?

a. There are a few good commercial pet foods
out there—look for ones that have not been
recalled and that have human-quality meat
and whole grains. They are okay, but home-
cooked is ideal.

Soon, there were reports that as many as 3,200 pets had
died from tainted food, mostly due to kidney failure; another 6,000 were said to have become ill. The recall involved
pet foods from more than one hundred separate brands, as
Menu was the provider of pet food components to several
centralized processing plants, including two in the United

States. In fact, Menu Foods makes private-label pet food for seventeen of the top 20 North American retailers, including Kroger, Safeway, and Wal-Mart.

But the recall was by no means confined to cheaper, mass-market brands: also pulled off the shelves were top-of-the-line brands like Iams and Eukanuba. Pet owners were understandably worried, and remain so. Since the original recall, melamine has been found in rice gluten and corn gluten, and the recall has broadened. Pet lovers around the country are very, very worried, not to mention angry:

* What have I been feeding my pet?

* What can I feed her now?

* What's gone so wrong?

My mission with this book is to help guide you through these uncertain times. I offer you my experience, my education and my lifelong passion for pets. Together, let's change the way we think about how we feed our beloved pets, and how we prepare for the future.

Joan Weiskopf
May 2007

Introduction

Family lore has it that when I was about a year old—before I had even taken my first step—I stood up out of my stroller and walked directly over to a big white fluffy dog and gave a toddler's hello. Apparently, the big white fluffy dog (which I now know was a Great Pyrenees) greeted my wobbly approach with benign amusement.

Good doggie!

Thus began my life-long fascination with animals. Fifty years later I am still in thrall to our four-legged friends; in fact, I remain particularly enamored of big white fluffy dogs, as professionally I breed, train, and show Bedlington terriers, who are fluffy and white, although nowhere near the size of my first Great Pyrenees friend.

My early years were spent in the busy New York City borough of Queens. Our family moved when I was three to New Rochelle, a quiet bedroom community with large houses, wide, tree-lined streets, and plenty of backyards. I got a new little brother I loved but no dog, and one of my earliest memories is that I set about to change that. I tried to adopt about every neighborhood mutt I could sweet-talk into my company. One day—I couldn't have been more than four or five—a cocker spaniel named Georgia and I ran away from home. Every policeman in the area was on alert to pick me up and take me back to my parents. And they did. More than once. I don't remember where I wanted to go. I wasn't unhappy. I just knew I was happiest when wandering around in the company of my sweet canine neighbor, Georgia.

When I was about twelve we *finally* got our own dog, a miniature poodle named Jiffi. We named her Jiffi because I was Joan, Mom was Janet, Dad was Jesse, and my brother was Jay. It had to be a J.

Q. Should I stop feeding my cat commercial pet food immediately?

A. No pet diet should be changed suddenly. All change should be gradual—7 to 10 days for a complete change.

For all intents and purposes, Jiffi was mine. I had been relentless in wanting to get a pet, and it was a reward for something commendable I did but that is now lost to memory. Perhaps I cleaned my room. (Unlikely.) In any event, "the dog" was my responsibility. "The dog's your responsibility, Joanie," my mother would say. But she didn't have to remind me often.

Unlike many other teenagers, I fulfilled my responsibilities to Jiffi loyally, faithfully, happily.

I loved that dog.

Much of what I learned about dealing with pets I learned early:

Listen to them.
Watch them.
Learn about them.
Feed them well.

Feeding back then (the late 1950s) was much different from today. Most people treated their pets as an additional household member, as they do now, and they fed them accordingly. There wasn't much specialty food—pet food—available. The grocery store aisles were not lined up with dog and cat food.

We fed them from our kitchens.

I remember my mother going to the butcher shop once a month to stock the family freezer with meat. After ordering everything we needed—chops and roasts and fryers and sausages and steaks—she'd ask for some "dog meat." The kindly butcher would then produce a log of ground, frozen trimmings from his walk-in freezer. How much, Ma'am? the butcher would ask, poised with his saw in the air. My mother would order several 1-pound chunks sawed from the log, and that would be the main food source for Jiffy for a good month, complemented by table scraps and whatever else she could talk people into giving her.

In 1968 I went to college at the University of Illinois to study pre-veterinary medicine. I loved the work and the science and the prospect of working with dogs and cats (I also loved cats), but unfortunately, the administrators at the vet school did not look kindly on women entering the program. It may come as a surprise to many, but back then, most vet programs were for guys, and they centered on what I call "chain food medicine," that is, large-animal veterinary practice. Small-animal disciplines were mostly an aside.

Needless to say, I switched majors, to fine arts, mostly metalworking and jewelry design. I felt these made for more practical career choices, given the hippie 1960s and the reality then of the vet school landscape, as it had related to me in no uncertain terms. I graduated from Illinois with dual degrees in fine arts and medical illustration in 1972 and went on to Rochester Institute of Technology, where I earned a master's degree in teaching. I worked in the jewelry industry for many, many years.

In 1977, I got the first dog of my own as an adult: Percy, a Bedlington terrier, the breed commonly referred to as lamblike. I got him from a breeder I knew in New Jersey. The curves and line and the sculpture-like qualities of that particular terrier attracted me and has held my heart ever since.

From that point on I was hooked. My journey since then has led me to write this very book.

Unfortunately, Percy was a sickly dog. I discovered that Bedlington terriers have a serious genetic flaw that makes them prone to liver toxicosis (in humans this is called Wilson's disease). Medically, Percy was missing the enzyme required to metabolize copper. Copper, though needed only in trace quantities, is present in drinking water (thanks to copper pipes), but if your system doesn't have the key to breaking it down, it builds up in your liver and will reach poisonous levels. Thankfully, a medicine called penicillamine came along, which chelates (binds) the copper and flushes it from the system. I was amazed to see the application of good science and intelligent intervention up close.

My interest and fascination with veterinary medicine returned full force. At the age of thirty-five I resolved to finish what I had started back in Illinois, or at least try.

Of the twenty-seven vet schools in the country, the only one that had a significant interest in animal nutrition was Tufts in Boston. There I came to understand that my true calling lay in prevention of health problems in animals, rather than in tending to the sick or injured.

After leaving Tufts, I did all I could to learn about alternative methods of care, including feeding. I developed a network of vets and pet owners who were able to give me some very good information on nutritional care for dogs.

Q.: What's better: canned or dry pet food?

Q.: Because the canning process itself is a preserving process, there are fewer chemical preservatives in canned food, unless your dry food manufacturer is diligent about using natural preservatives. Read the label!

Today, I live in Pennsylvania with my six adult dogs, all Bedlingtons. My "kennel" is a black leather sofa in the living room. I cook for my dogs every day. But that's just me.

I don't expect every pet owner to be at the stove for their doggies and kitties every day, or to give over their household furniture to their pets. Our lives can be hectic, our schedules cramped, and there are so many options for feeding your pet. But as a breeder, dog show person, and lover of animals who knows just a little about how dogs work, I do want to share with you how my experience is reflected in my feeding regimen, if only to show you how much loving care can be put—and easily put—into tending your beloved furry friends.

The Way I Feed My Dogs

Every morning, I let the dogs out, let them in, and feed them breakfast. Sometimes I have prepared some meals in advance and frozen them; sometimes I cook them up fresh. It all depends on my schedule.

Regardless, this is the regimen I follow.

Five days a week, they will get either chicken livers or chicken hearts or chicken gizzards, which I buy in bulk every two months—fifty pounds' worth, organic and free range (of course, I freeze a good deal of it), which brings the cost to a little over one hundred dollars. That's breakfast for six for six to eight weeks.

The chicken parts I sauté very lightly in organic coconut oil. I sauté the chicken giblets only enough to take off the chill; the middle is completely raw. I add string beans (fresh or frozen, not canned—too much sodium) to the skillet and zucchini, which you can get fresh all year round. In the winter months, I put some grain in the breakfast—cooked oatmeal or barley, pasta, couscous, kasha, or brown rice.

I scoop it into their bowls, almost always adding a fish oil capsule and a heaping teaspoon of organic full-fat yogurt. I refresh their water.

The other two mornings, I fix them eggs—scrambled eggs: four eggs for my six terriers.

At around 11:30, my dogs start looking at the refrigerator, as if it might magically open under their steady, loyal gaze. It does get opened, by me, and I give them each a raw chicken neck—dipped first in boiling water to kill any surface bacteria but without cooking the nutrients out of the bones within.

For dinner, they get the boiled chicken (or rabbit, duck, bison, venison, lamb, hamburger, pork, or fish twice a week; all pets, dogs and cats, need their protein sources varied). I give them whatever vegetables are in season (broccoli, cabbage, kale, romaine, carrots occasionally, sweet potatoes occasionally, asparagus, green peppers), all lightly sautéed in the chicken juices. I may toss a little rice or some kind of cooked grain in as well.

Q.: My dog has eaten some chocolate. How do I know if he has eaten too much?

Q.: Symptoms of chocolate toxicity are vomiting, diarrhea, panting, restlessness, increased urination, and muscle tremors.

Domesticated cats and dogs should not be grazing, so I pick the bowls up off the floor after a half hour (if there is ever any food left). These animals have made their kills, now it's time for them to rest. No snacks till bedtime, when—I shouldn't say this—I might indulge them with a potato chip or, more healthfully, some air-popped popcorn. They are likely to receive gifts of fruit daily, like bananas, pineapple, apples, or melon (but never grapes). Dried fruits are fine: dates, figs, apricots (but never raisins).

Myth

Too much fat is bad for dogs and cats.

The Truth: Dogs and cats metabolize fats differently than humans do. Fats provide thermo-regulation and energy. Unless there is some other underlying disease process, fats are good for our pets, especially Omega 3 from fish.

In *Pet Food Nation,* I hope to show you just how easy and inexpensive it is to ensure that your dog or cat is eating nutritiously—whether you are cooking for one or six, for a malamute or a beagle, for a Persian or a Maine Coon cat; whether you are relying to some extent on commercial pet food or table scraps, or a mixture. The most important thing to understand is your own pet. Once you realize what he or she needs—specific to breed, geography, age, and temperament—you'll never need to worry that you aren't doing the best for your pet. But if it's commercial pet food you're using, to whatever extent, you'll have to learn to read the label! You have brought your pets into your world. They deserve the best you can give them. And they need it now more than ever.

Special note: Transitioning to a Healthy Diet

If this book or events in general inspire you to make a change in your pet's diet, please do so gradually, over seven to ten days, introducing a little bit more of the new diet each day. A change for the better often fails if done too quickly. The pet can experience a variety of problems, including diarrhea, excessive urination, and possible kidney failure. Be careful, be slow, be patient. Good health is not far away.

Here's why your pet may very well need such a change.

part one

Why You Need This Book Now

The Pet Food Scandal

lthough it is true that the spring 2007 recall was the largest in the history of the pet food industry, it is by no means the first time tainted pet food has caused a problem.

In late 2005, the presence of aflatoxin forced a manufacturer to recall its product; in the past year, traces of aminopterin, used in rat poison, were found in dog food that turned deadly. Back in 1995, Nature's Recipe pulled $20 million worth of its product due to the presence of vomitoxin; the source of that recall has not been conclusively identified. Melamine, although not meant to be in food, is not known to be toxic. Some suspect that melamine found in the 2007 products is a "marker" for something else that is proving deadly, as yet unidentified. If that is the case, perhaps the melamine is not even necessary to the fatal tainting of pet food. No wonder pet owners are nervous; no wonder the pet food industry is nervous, too.

I hope to be able to give some relief by explaining what's at stake and what the issues are.

Q.: Is milk/dairy really good for cats, even as a special treat?

A.: Cats lose the ability to digest lactose, but a small amount as a treat is fine if they tolerate it. Best to use a fermented milk product, such as yogurt, kefir (fermented cow's milk), or buttermilk, which have great health benefits from the good bacteria it puts into the system.

There are an estimated 144 million pet cats and dogs in the United States; their owners bought more than $15 billion worth of pet food last year. That's a lot of kibble. But with the threat of deadly illness hanging in the air, pet owners cannot wait for the industry or its regulators at the FDA to step in and tell them what's wrong and how it is to be fixed. There's no time, and there's too much at stake.

There is one thing, however, that pet owners can do that will not only ensure the nutritional health of their companion animals *right now,* but in all likelihood will radically transform (and reform) the pet food industry itself: *make their own pet food.* For those of you who want to try, read on. For those of you who fear that it might be impractical to make your own pet food, also please read on: you will learn how to read a commercial pet food label and know just what you are giving your pet.

A Canned History of the Pet Food Industry

Before you make up your mind about how you intend to feed your pet today, tomorrow, or into the future, let me first give you a brief overview of the pet food business. It's good to be informed—and you may well conclude that the recent scandal was less an aberration than an inevitability.

Although the 2007 pet food scandal has grabbed the attention of the mass media and has understandably come as a shock to many pet owners, concerned animal nutrition advocates have been warning for years that mass-produced pet food was potentially harmful to pets, and certainly not healthy for them. Much of the problem stems from the fact that dogs and cats are carnivores; they need significant amounts of protein in their diets. Protein is not easily come by and is subject to bacterial decay; hence, ensuring uncontaminated food as well as long shelf life is a challenge.

Myth

A pet eating grass is a sign of sickness.

The Truth: Ingesting grasses and dirt is more likely to mean that your pet is in need of some varied nutrients. Good soil, for example, contains micronutrients; weeds and grasses, especially dandelion, can be very good liver cleansers. Of course, any chemically treated plant or grass is not good. Grass eating, unless excessive or followed by vomiting, is a good thing.

It is well known that pet food companies, in their search for protein, have resorted to slaughterhouse waste, restaurant grease, and garbage, not to mention the four Ds: dead, diseased, dying, and disabled animals.

To ensure that there is no bacteria in these components, they are rendered—that is, cooked in a vat (hair, hoof, collars, plastic bags, and all) at about 250 degrees for up to an hour, then centrifuged at high speeds till the tallow floats to the top. The tallow is used as a source of fat in pet foods and sprayed on chunks to make them tastier to the animals; some of the rest may be processed into kibble. This cooking indeed kills bacteria, but it also eliminates all the healthy enzymes found in meat products. And the high heat and centrifuging does not remove heavy chemicals, like the sodium pentobarbital that is used to euthanize animals. Likewise, the grain elements used in pet foods (unless labeled "whole grains") come from more or less the bottom silage, the sweepings from farm silos, where disinfectants and metals mix with the grain dust and husks, and the grain itself is subject to contamination by a variety of mycotoxins.

The low-rent sources for much of what constitutes commercial pet food is alarming enough, but with the rendering of protein compromising nutritional value and the high toxin exposure of the grain sources, a pet owner might be excused for, well, gagging.

Q. What is rendering?

A. Rendering is when raw materials are dumped into a large vat and boiled for several hours to separate fat, remove water, and kill bacteria, viruses, and parasites. The high temperatures used (270°F/130°C) can destroy natural enzymes and proteins found in the raw ingredients. Then there are myriad chemicals sprayed on the food to prevent toxic mold buildup. Instead of toxic mold, the pet food contains toxic chemicals!

It was not always thus. Cats and dogs have been domesticated as both working animals and pets for thousands of years (dogs much longer than cats, however). Until less than a hundred years ago, cats and dogs for the most part relied on a diet of prey, table scraps, and food from the butcher or the fisherman. They ate the ends of bread, oatmeal, and barley from the scrapings of the family pot, and bits of fruit;

they chewed on bones left over from family meals. They drank clean water and milk and buttermilk slurry.

In fact, there wasn't even a pet food industry until the late 19th century, and it was hardly an industry.

A man named James Spratt, an American entrepreneur trying to sell lightning rods, ventured to London in search of customers. He brought his dog along with him; on the transatlantic passage the dog was given some old ship biscuits, the bane of many a sailor's diet and, Spratt decided, not worthy of his dog. But it give Spratt an idea: to develop a dog cake that was nutritious and edible. Spratt's Patent was founded. Spratt's biscuit consisted of ground wheat, vegetables, beetroot, and dried meat, including buffalo imported from America. He started his company in England, where there was a considerable demand from English country gentlemen with hunting dogs and mastiffs. He began a U.S. operation in the 1890s, setting up shop in Newark, New Jersey.

Spratt and a few other British companies dominated the small market in the early decades of the twentieth century, until F. H. Bennett of New York City introduced the "milk bone biscuit," a calcium-fortified staple. Bennett eventually made dozens of varieties of biscuits and crackers, but his great innovation was to make the biscuit in the shape of a bone. Dogs ate it up.

Many innovators followed: P. M. Chappel began canning

dog food in the 1920s under the Ken-L-Ration brand; what they canned was horse meat, which met with a rocky reception at first, but, when dogs proved to love it, was eventually accepted. Clarence Gaines introduced a dry formula and also engineered a national distribution network. It was only a matter of time before a national-brand food purveyor of human food got into the act. In 1931 the National Biscuit Company (Nabisco) bought Milk Bone, which resulted in a sales force 3,000 strong calling on the nation's storeowners to stock what they heretofore had not: food for animals.

Q. I pay top dollar to buy high-quality dry cat food with no animal by-products for my pet. Am I correct in assuming that this is safe food and good for her, especially since the brand is not on the recall list?

A. Almost all commercially prepared kibble (dry food) is grain-based. It would be better to feed the cat a home-prepared diet of seventy-five percent animal-based protein.

Today, pet food companies are huge, and the past few years have seen large companies bought up by even larger ones. Nestlé's bought Purina to form Nestlé Purina; it produces the well-known Fancy Feast, Alpo, Friskies, Mighty Dog, Puppy Chow, and Tender Vittles. Del Monte bought the pet food division of Heinz, now home to Gravy Train, 9Lives, MeowMix, and Nature's Recipe. Mars Inc. acquired the Royal Canin line, which includes Pedigree, Waltham's, and Sensible Choice, and just lately gobbled up Nutro. Procter and Gamble (P&G) bought the well-respected Iams company, maker of Iams and Eukanuba, nearly eight years ago, and Colgate-Palmolive got into the business by acquiring the venerable Hill's Science Diet. Then, of course, there are many boutique and private-label pet food companies.

One of the things made patently clear in the latest recall is that labels large and small get ingredients from one of three gigantic co-packagers—and then affix their own labels. When the list of recalled lines runs one hundred deep, nearly everyone is implicated. Not all, of course, but consumers must beware.

But why beware when you can simply prepare?

In most homes, the foods are present that can nutritiously feed the family cat or dog. Although for many years vets advised against feeding pets "human food," you seldom hear that now. Instead, you will hear the proviso "But you must supplement with vitamins and enzymes and be careful not to feed them too much of one thing or not enough of another."

Of course. As with humans, achieving a healthy balanced diet is *not* a no-brainer. You have to think a little. But once you have understood the needs of your particular pet and committed to a regimen of food and supplements, it will become second nature. It won't be as mindless as opening a can or picking up the fifty-pound bag at the supermarket and filling the water bowl twice a day; rather, it will become an extension of your love for your pet.

If you can do it, you should.

If you can't, if you must rely on commercial pet food, do it right.

Who's Minding the Store?

The effects of a half-century of burgeoning pet ownership has spawned a big business in pet food. And with big business comes salesmanship. It is the salesmanship that has exacted a price.

In the competition for business from pet owners, pet food manufacturers have done their best to sell you their products, making claims for the delectability and nutritional value of their food. In that effort, they have searched for larger markets and greater margins, as most any business would. Unfortunately, and unlike the food industry in general, the oversight for the food we feed our pets has been weak, as the tainted pet food scare has shown.

Who is the watchdog when it comes to pet food? Well, let's be honest: it's not the kind of watchdog you'd want guarding anything precious to you. But you should know who they are.

Three organizations oversee the industry. The federal Food and Drug Administration (FDA), the Center for Veterinary Medicine (CVM), and the Association of American Feed Control Officials (AAFCO). What's missing here? Think about who inspects the beef you eat and the chicken you buy for your family. That's the Department of Agriculture, and the Department of Agriculture is involved only in the pet food that we export outside of the country. Inside our borders, we have only the FDA. Now the FDA hardly has pet food at the center of its radar screen; it is a federal agency that regulates, among other things, drugs, medical instruments, vaccines, blood products, and a lot of personal devices and appliances that emit radiation, such as cell phones and microwaves. The FDA farms out its pet food oversight responsibilities to the Center for Veterinary Medicine, a division of the FDA.

The CVM regulates the manufacture and distribution of food additives and drugs for pets. It has no role in monitoring where the food comes from—neither the proteins nor the fats nor the grains nor the water in pet food. The CVM is charged with upholding a requirement that the pet food be "pure and wholesome" and be truthfully labeled. Unfortunately, the CVM does little, if any, testing. It busies itself with, on occasion, attempting to verify exception claims made by a pet food manufacturer—"prevents worms," for example.

Fun Fact

What do the numbers 310807, 083107, and 8/31/07 have in common? They are accepted notations of "best before" dates on pet food; the first is in the International Date Code style.

The regulation of pet food labeling falls to the AAFCO, which works in partnership with the FDA and CVM. Many could persuasively argue that this is a case of the fox minding the chicken coop, as the AAFCO is little more than a trade organization, whose membership includes representatives from the large pet food manufacturers. That is not to say that the AAFCO does not have pet health clearly in mind; after all, the pet food industry needs our pets (more than our pets need them!). The AAFCO issues, no doubt in good faith, a vast and complicated array of labeling requirements, beginning with what requirements must be met to allow a manufacturer to say "All Chicken" or "Fish Platter" or "With Beef" on the bag or can. But it has no teeth. Its requirements are really more in the way of standards. Manufacturers are supposed to meet those standards, but, as with the CVM, there is little or no testing going on.

Thus, today we have to trust ourselves and common sense. There is a world of information about what you might be feeding your pet. It's up to you to find it. My hope is that this book makes that job easier.

part two

What Your Pet Wants You to Know

Sound Nutrition for Your Pet

When it comes to understanding our pet cats and dogs, it's crucial to understand where they came from. Their origins and history as a species, combined with the more recent histories of their breeding and the customs of their care, are what determine what they need today.

Both cats and dogs began as predators in the wild; both are classified as carnivores—that is, their metabolism depends on meat protein and they are built and wired to acquire it and process it. It is how they grow. A 2002 study published in the journal *Science* examined the mitochondrial DNA of dogs found at archaeological sites around the world and concluded that dogs descended from wolves in East Asia, where they were first domesticated. This theory has superseded previous beliefs that the dog originated in the Middle East. In any event, it is likely that wild wolves in search of food were attracted to human encampments, attracted by the smells of food being prepared. The wilder, flightier dogs may have shied away, while the more passive members of a wild pack may have lingered around the settlements, eventually finding that their presence was welcome, with food coming a little easier. Of course, with their speed, strength, and sharp teeth, early dogs were excellent hunters. It was only a matter of time before those dogs who found human company hospitable were eventually trained to help in the hunting. These animals accompanied humans on long travels across Asia and across the Bering Strait, bringing the species to the Americas some 12,000 to 15,000 years ago.

Although hunter-gatherers were responsible for spreading dogs across the world, it was the development of permanently sited farming cultures that led to the true domestication of the animals, with selective breeding. Since dogs were found to be instrumental in a variety of important community functions—hunting, birding, waterfowl retrieval, herding, vermin control, not to mention serving as guards and companions—the variety of combinations of breeding to isolate one or more of these virtues led to the enormous variety within the species that we have today.

The origins of today's cat are less in dispute. They are descended from the African wildcat *(Felis sylvestris lybica)*. A small, fast animal that roamed in the African savannas, the African wildcat descended from early miacids, as are lions and tigers. The domestication of cats (into *Felis sylvestris catus)* is thought to have begun only 4,000 years ago, in Egypt, where their mysterious ways were a source of fascination and their ability to hunt down rodents most welcome. The fact that the cat has been domesticated for far less time than the dog explains a lot—about the independence and strong will we attribute to the felines, as opposed to the dog's widely cherished sociability. The cat's diet is also closer to what it was in the wild than is the dog's. Cats are considered not only carnivores but "obligate" carnivores, meaning they *must* have animal protein (whereas a dog can survive longer on a low-protein diet). The cat's methodical and deadly stalking and pouncing are well known. Even today, cats who have never been off the living room carpet, if left to their own devices on the street or in a meadow would not go hungry. The same cannot be said for the dog, though the social charm of most canines will go a long way toward getting them what they need, at least for a while.

> *Q.* Since dogs and cats descend from prey animals and are accustomed to feasting on their kill and then resting till hungry again, should I also occasionally make my pet fast?
>
> *Q.* No. Unless your pet is on a raw food diet (which I don't recommend), fasting is not a good idea. In fact, cats, who get most of their water from food, should never go long without eating—never an entire day.

What does this tell us, in general, about our pets? First of all, it tells us that our pets are descended from species that ate raw food: animal meat, organs, bone, blood, even hair, fur, and feathers. Both cats and dogs were locked into finding protein, so that eggs, reptiles, and rodents were on the menu. More so than cats, dogs are believed to have eaten carrion; they would eat from carcasses they found in the woods. Dogs were also more likely to feast on the digestive tracks of killed or found prey, thereby often ingesting grain and vegetable matter from non-carnivorous prey, such as deer.

Being hunters, cats and dogs are also, in their origins, feast-and-famine animals. That is, they gorge on kill, then rest to digest and only move again when hungry. Since hunters are eating raw food, this cycle allows them to complete the process of digestion and evacuation of waste before having another fill, an important factor in avoiding bacterial infection.

Finally, we should note that the African wildcat, being a grassland animal, was not accustomed to an abundance of available water; cats today, it is plain to see, are hardly built for lapping up water like a dog is. As a result, cats absorb virtually all the moisture they need from their prey—or their pet food.

Q.: Some of my fancy friends are now giving their dogs and cats bottled water to drink. Is this ridiculous or recommended?

Q.: Tap water is just as harmful for your pet as it is for you. Bottled, filtered, or reverse-osmosis water is a great investment.

So what should we do? Simple: We should feed our pets with their ancestral feeding habits in mind. If you give your cat a mouse, give your dog a rabbit.

The Pet Food Pie

Of course, it's a little impractical in these times to have your animals feed on live prey, but it has not always been so. A hundred years ago, cats and dogs, though welcome in homes, basically foraged for themselves. Water and table scraps might be left for them on the back porch, but as often as not, looking for Puss or King was futile as they were out on hunting expeditions.

It's a different world today.

Still, the nutrients your dog or cat was ingesting in its self-caught meal is what we must discover in order to provide a healthy diet. What were our African wildcat and East

Asian dog getting on their forays into woods or fields? Six things, which make up the pet food pie:

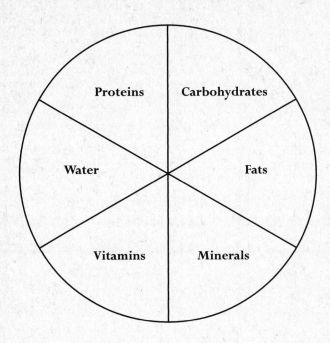

The correct proportions of these elements is the source of not only some dispute, but of confusing ways of measurement: by weight, by volume, by calorie? The standard way of listing ingredients is by weight, but that doesn't break out the value of some of the nutrients, such as protein and fat, that might reside in more than one type of ingredient (meat has protein and so do grains, for example). My rule of thumb is that cats should have seventy-five percent protein and the rest in grains, vegetables, and fruit, while the dog ratio should be sixty-five percent protein, with the balance in grains, vegetables, and fruit. For both, an occasional multivitamin supplement is a good idea.

Q.: When the pet food label says "meat," what animal is it from?

A.: "Meat" refers only to skeletal muscle tissue taken from cows, swine, sheep, and goats. Since sheep and goats are rare compared to the 37 million cows and 100 million hogs slaughtered for food every year, nearly all meat by-products come from cattle and pigs.

Essential Components of the Pet Animal Diet

1) **Protein:** Protein is found in both animal and plant material, specifically grains. Meat, poultry, dairy, and eggs are high-quality sources of protein; rice barley, wheat, rye, and

corn are good sources of vegetable protein, but the vegetable and grain proteins are of lesser quality than animal protein. Cats need more protein, perhaps twice as much as dogs.

2) Carbohydrates: Our pets and we differ greatly in the need for carbohydrates and in how we digest them. Our pets' need for carbs can be completely satisfied by their diet and synthesis in their bodies, provided that the diet has adequate protein and fat. Starches and grains are virtually useless to our pets unless they are well cooked. Just remember that commercial pet foods may contain thirty to sixty percent dry-weight carbs in dry food, and five to thirty percent in wet canned food.

3) Fats: Animal fat is a great source of energy for cats and dogs and carries essential fatty acids. Fats also help transport fat-soluble vitamins (which the body stores more easily than water-soluble vitamins) throughout the body. They also make food taste better and stimulate appetite. Fats are also found in some vegetables (lots in avocados) and some fruits (dates) and are in good supply in nuts and seeds.

4) Vitamins: There are two categories of vitamins: water-soluble and fat-soluble. Water-soluble vitamins include the

B vitamins, niacin, pantothenic acid, folic acid, biotin, choline, and Vitamin C. Fat-soluble vitamins are Vitamins A, D, E, and K.

5) Minerals: Minerals are essential for bone formation, muscle metabolism, fluid balance, and nervous system function. Major essential minerals are potassium, calcium, phosphorus, magnesium, and sodium chloride. Trace elements are iron, copper, manganese, zinc, iodine, selenium, and cobalt. Although mineral dietary requirements are minimal, they are essential to general good health.

6) Water: Clean, fresh water is essential to nearly every process of your pet's body. Neither cat nor dog can last more than a few days without water. Cats ancestrally are accustomed to absorbing their water from their prey. In today's world, it's best to keep a bowl filled for them. Same for doggie.

Whatever you feed your pet, and from wherever it comes, it should aspire to represent all six parts of the pet food pie. Otherwise, you're doing your pet wrong.

The Balanced Diet

Most books that break down the proper diet for dogs and cats are going to be misleading. They will likely say that a dog diet should consist of one-third protein, one-third grains and carbohydrates, and one-third fruits and vegetables. For cats, they will recommend two-thirds protein and the rest in grains, carbs, and fruit. This can be misleading because it assumes you are feeding your pets commercial pet food, where the animal protein is generally of low quality and much of the protein is therefore provided through grains. Dogs on a diet of homemade pet food could do well with having three-fourths of their diet be animal source by weight. That would give them not only all the protein they need, but all the fats and carbs and most of the vita-mins and minerals as well, and in a highly bioavailable form—meaning they can easily absorb it. If making your own pet food is not your first choice, then just make sure as best you can that the animal protein is of the highest quality you can get in a commercially available pet food.

Food Groups and Sources

It is important to know the nutritional yield of various food groups. Below is an ideal yield from organic product. The numbers will be somewhat compromised by many commercial pet food processes.

Meat: All meats yield similar amounts of protein (6 to 8 grams per ounce). Lamb, pork, and beef are highest in fat; poultry is lowest. Lamb yields the most calcium, poultry the least. Beef kidney and poultry are the lowest in calories.

Dairy: Per cup, cottage cheese trumps all other dairy in protein (26 grams); plain yogurt yields 12 grams and has half the fat. Note that fat is not bad for your pet unless your vet has determined that it has a weight problem. Cottage cheese, however, is loaded with salt, even low-sodium brands.

Grains: Couscous and pasta have the most protein, about 9 grams per cooked cup. Oats, brown rice, and rye are high in calcium. Oats and whole wheat are high in potassium. Corn, barley, and rye are highest in fiber.

Vegetables: Black beans, lentils, and lima beans are the kings of vegetable protein—though legumes (watch out for soybeans) can cause digestive problems. I recommend against using any soy product: tofu, sprouts, beans. Vegetables are great sources of potassium, except for a few, such as artichokes and green peppers. As for vitamins, broccoli, parsley, and spinach are very high in A and C.

Fruits: The main dietary value of fruits is in providing vitamins, minerals, fiber, and enzymes. Dates and figs are surprisingly good sources of protein and fat, as well as calcium. But raisins and grapes—No!

Nuts and seeds: Sunflower seeds are high in calories and fat and provide some calcium. Pecans also have a good amount of fat and are loaded with calcium. Nuts and seeds should be ground or chopped for any pet, or little of the nutritional benefit will be absorbed. Almonds are the best— they should always be raw, unsalted, and preferably organic.

Should I Use
Commercial Pet Food?

ow that you have a basic outline of what your pet, whether dog or cat, needs, it's time to ask the question: Do I feed my boon companion a commercial variety of pet food?

The safest—and, at the moment, sanest—answer to the question is *No!* The recent pet food recall has shaken not only pet owners; it has shaken a multibillion-dollar industry to its core. You better believe that the commercial pet food business is gravely concerned, not only about the quality of its product, but about maintaining (the loyalty of) its customers. With the number of cats and dogs in America approaching 150 million, this is serious business indeed. Those pets are going to be fed. The question is, what will they be fed and who will make it?

As we know, the methods of producing commercial pet food are not regulated in the way that the production and packaging of human food is. As we also know, the regulations that are in place—most of them subject only to voluntary compliance—cannot easily or effectively be extended to some of the basic components that come from overseas. Store-bought pet foods come in a variety of styles, at a variety of prices, and of varying quality. But the centralized distribution system exposed in the Menu Foods recall of 2007, where melamine-laced wheat gluten from China became a component in more than one hundred different brands, has called into question every consumer assumption about what we are paying for. Is the relatively high-quality Iams really healthier than some of the lower-priced foods? Or are only *some* of the components of better grade? One thing melamine (a by-product of coal used in fertilizer, but whose nitrogen levels can be misread as levels of protein) did was render every brand of pet food no stronger than its weakest (or most toxic) link.

Let's Be Real for a Minute

I don't give my pets commercial pet food. But when it comes to assessing the situation for other, understandably concerned pet owners, I am a realist. I realize that arguing for strict avoidance of anything of a commercial origin is impractical advice for many of us.

Not every person is going to want to feed his or her pet food from the table; not every person is going to have the time or inclination to prepare food. After all, many Americans, for a variety of reasons, don't even feed themselves very well, much less their four-legged companions. In addition, there are situations where even the most diligent of pet owners, those committed to the healthiest foods, find themselves, say, on a road trip with a hungry dog on board, at which point, lacking homemade provisions iced in a cooler, the passing supermarket might provide a couple of cans of acceptable food that'll suit Bowser in the backseat just fine.

Q. I have a busy young family and we travel a lot. We love to bring our Labrador with us. In a pinch, can you recommend any fast-food or drive-thru food that would be safe for our pet, since we often rely on that for ourselves?

A. No problem giving the dog a filet of fish (if possible, remove some of the coating). It's okay to feed a plain burger, leaving off the bun and the fixings. Chicken is fine in strips or pieces, again removing the coating if possible.

Reading the Label

Commercial pet food does have labeling requirements, all of which are contained in the annually revised official publication of the AAFCO. Although the AAFCO cannot be said to regulate the pet food industry, it does provide standards that pet food makers are expected to follow.

If you are currently feeding your pet from a bag or a can, I strongly recommend that you read the label, regardless of whether you plan to stick with commercial pet food or to transition to another feeding regimen. But before you get to the label, just look at the container itself. A lot is evident right there.

✳ *The name of the food:* This provides the first indication of the food's content. If it says **"All** Beef*"* or **"100%** Chicken,*"* the product cannot contain more than that one ingredient (aside from water and trace amounts of preservatives and condiments such as salt or onion powder).

✳ *Style of food:* Products labeled **Dinner** or **Recipe** or **Entrée** or **Platter** are bound by the AAFCO's "25% Rule," which applies when an ingredient constitutes at least 25 percent of the weight of a wet product or at least 10 percent of the dry matter. A combination of ingredients **(beef and lamb)** included in the product name is permissible when each ingredient constitutes at least 3 percent of the product weight, excluding water weight. If any product makes a point of saying **With Chicken** or **With Lamb,** the "with" ingredient must amount to at least 3 percent of the food by weight.

✳ *Flavors:* If a pet food is labeled as having a certain "flavor"—say, **Chicken Flavor**—the product itself need contain only a very small extract of chicken, or may even contain an artificial chicken flavor. It need not contain chicken itself.

✳ *Life stages:* Choosing the proper food got even more challenging when manufacturers started labeling their foods as being suited for certain life stages, such as puppy or kitten, large adult or senior. According to the AAFCO, the body that governs the standards for pet-food labeling, there are only two true designations: puppy and kitten. These formulas generally have more calories and protein. Products labeled for older cats and dogs generally are no different from regular adult formulas.

"Lite" formulas can be misleading. Many labels don't display calorie breakdowns. If you want to know the calorie count, contact the manufacturer. A pet food can claim to be "light" or "lean" only if it meets the AAFCO's standard definitions for these terms. These definitions differ for dog and cat food and also depend on the moisture content of the food. The words "light," "lite," and "low-calorie" all have the same meaning. The words "lean" and "low-fat" also mean the same. But "fewer calories" and "reduced calories" mean only that the product has fewer calories than another product, and "less fat" and "reduced fat" mean the product is less fatty than another one.

Ingredient Labeling

The ingredient list itself holds the key to what's actually in that pet food from a bag or can. Ingredients are listed in descending order of weight.

As we know, pets need protein, carbohydrates (grains,

vegetables), fat, minerals, and vitamins. But what they need most (cats somewhat more than dogs) is protein. The protein used in pet food comes from a variety of sources. When cattle, swine, chickens, lambs, or other animals are slaughtered, lean muscle tissue is trimmed away from the carcass for human consumption, along with the few organs that people like to eat, such as tongues and tripe. About fifty percent of every food animal does not get used in human foods. Whatever remains—head, feet, bones, blood, intestines, lungs, spleen, liver, ligaments, fat trimmings, and other parts not generally consumed by humans—is used in pet food, animal feed, fertilizer, industrial lubricants, soap, rubber, and other products. These "other parts" are known as "by-products."

Meat: When a label says "meat," it is referring to muscle, whether of mammal, poultry, or fish. Although it may be accompanied by fat, sinew, skin, and nerve, it comes directly from the slaughterhouse and has been somehow processed, though not rendered.

> $Q.$ Should dogs be allowed to chew bones?
>
> $A.$ Bones are fine if they are fresh and raw, with the exception of chicken and fish bones, but *never* give cooked bones of any kind. The marrow from a fresh, raw bone is good for the dog or cat, but too much can cause diarrhea. Scoop some of it out for another day.

Meat by-product: The thing to look out for in commercial pet food is "meat by-product." According to the AAFCO, "Meat by-product is the nonrendered, clean parts of slaughtered mammals other than meat." Basically, it is animal parts that are not meat; it can be lungs, kidneys, brains, spleens, intestines, blood, and livers, all of which are likely repositories for a variety of diseased tissues and contaminants. In poultry, by-product can include heads and feet. You seldom see fish by-product, but see below for fish meal. Some people argue that, because a carnivorous prey animal, cat or dog, would be accustomed to eating plenty of "meat by-product" (hair, feather, hooves, intestines, waste matter), there is no cause for alarm. True, if you could trust that all commercial meat by-products were healthy. But the origin of much of this meat by-product in commercial pet foods—zoo animals, euthanized pets and horses, often old and diseased animals—makes meat by-product a less than welcome ingredient.

Meat meal: Meal, like by-product, is an iffy proposition in your pet food. It consists of product from mammalian tissue, such as blood, hoof, hide, hair, and even manure. The term "meal" means that these materials are not used fresh, but have been rendered.

Other protein sources: Some of the other sources of protein you don't want to know about, but you must if you take seriously the notion of buying commercial pet food. According to the AAFCO, these might very well be part of the protein component in your pet food: hair, spray-dried animal blood, dehydrated food waste (food garbage picked up from restaurants, etc.), dried paunch products (stomach contents of slaughtered cows), and dried swine waste.

Vegetable protein: Most dry foods contain a large amount of cereal grain or starchy vegetables to provide texture. These high-carbohydrate plant products also provide a cheap source of "energy"—the rest of us call it "calories." Gluten meals are high-protein extracts from which most of the carbohydrate has been removed. They are often used to boost protein percentages without expensive animal-source ingredients. Corn gluten meal is the most commonly used for this purpose. Wheat gluten is also used to create shapes like cuts, bites, chunks, shreds, flakes, and slices, and as a thickener for gravy. In most cases, foods containing vegetable proteins are among the poorer quality foods.

Q. I am a strict vegetarian (vegan) who owns two dogs (rescues). I feed them primarily vegetarian organic dry food and soy-based fake meats, which they love. Is this safe? They seem happy and healthy.

A. It is not a good idea to impose your vegan ways on any carnivore; soy products are not well digested by dogs and can cause bloating.

Animal and poultry fat: The unique, pungent odor you smell when you open a new bag of dry pet food—that's the smell of rendered animal fat, or vegetable fats and oils often deemed inedible by humans. These fats are sprayed directly onto extruded kibble and pellets to make them more palatable. The fat also acts as a binding agent to which manufacturers add other flavor enhancers, such as "animal digests" made from processed by-products.

Preservatives: Dog food companies are making moves to get away from using artificial preservatives. Chemicals used as preservatives, such as BHA, BHT, and ethoxyquin, have been under scrutiny, and many companies are switching to natural preservatives like Vitamin C (ascorbate), Vitamin E (tocopherols), and oils of rosemary, clove, or other spices to preserve the fats in their products.

Potential contaminants: Given the types of things manufacturers put in pet food, it is not surprising that bad things sometimes happen. Ingredients used in pet food are often highly contaminated with a wide variety of toxic substances. Some of these are destroyed by processing, but others are not.

Bacteria: Slaughtered animals, as well as those that have died because of disease, injury, or natural causes, are sources of meat, by-products, and rendered meals. An animal that died on the farm might not reach a rendering plant until days after its death. Therefore, the carcass is often contaminated with bacteria such as salmonella and E. coli. Pet food manufacturers do not test their products for bacterial endotoxins.

Chemicals: Because sick or dead animals can be processed as pet foods, the drugs that were used to treat or euthanize them may still be present in the end product. Penicillin and pentobarbital are just two examples of drugs that can pass through processing unchanged. Antibiotics used in livestock production are also thought to contribute to antibiotic resistance in humans.

Mycotoxins: Toxins from mold or fungi are called mycotoxins. Modern farming practices, adverse weather conditions, and improper drying and storage of crops can contribute to mold growth. Pet food ingredients that are most likely to be contaminated with mycotoxins are grains such as wheat and corn and fish meal.

How Is Pet Food Made?

The vast majority of dry food is made with a machine called an extruder. First, materials are blended in accordance with a recipe created with the help of computer programs that provide the nutrient content of each proposed ingredient. For instance, corn gluten meal has more protein than wheat flour. Because the extruder needs a consistent amount of starch and low moisture to work properly, dry ingredients— such as rendered meat and bone meal, poultry by-product meal, grains, and flours—predominate.

The dough is fed into the screws of an extruder. It is subjected to steam and high pressure as it is pushed through dies that determine the shape of the final product, much like the nozzles used in cake decorating. As the hot, pressurized dough exits the extruder, it is cut by a set of rapidly whirling knives into tiny pieces. As the dough reaches normal air pressure, it expands or "puffs" into its final shape. The food is allowed to dry, and then is usually sprayed with fat, digests, or other compounds to make it more palatable. When it is cooled, it can be bagged.

Semi-moist foods and many pet treats are also made with an extruder. To be appealing to consumers and to keep their texture, they contain many additives, colorings, and preservatives; they are not a good choice for a pet's primary diet.

Wet Food or Dry?

Wet or canned food begins with ground ingredients mixed with additives. If chunks are required, an extruder forms them. Then the mixture is cooked and canned. The sealed cans are then put into containers resembling pressure cookers, and commercial sterilization takes place. Some manufacturers cook the food right in the can.

Wet foods are quite different in content from dry or semi-moist foods. Although many canned foods contain by-products of various sorts, they are "fresh" and heavily processed (and they are often frozen for transport and storage). Wet foods usually contain much more protein, and it's often of a little higher quality, than dry foods. They also have more moisture, which is better for cats. They are packaged in cans or pouches.

Some Rules of Thumb for Commercial Pet Food Users

If you are going to buy commercial pet food, here are a few rules to follow:

1) Look for certification by the AAFCO. According to the FDA's Center for Veterinary Medicine, "An AAFCO nutritional adequacy statement is one of the most important aspects of a dog or cat food label." As I said, the AAFCO's independence as a consumer protector is not pristine, but this is the minimum you should require of your commercial pet food.

2) Look for meats that are human grade. The designation "USDA" means the product is approved for human consumption. Better yet, look for meat labeled "organic"; otherwise, the product is likely to contain hormones, growth stimulants, and antibiotics and/or may come from diseased and decayed animal flesh that just might even be cat or dog.

3) For cat and dog food, "meat" should be the first item listed. And skip anything that says "by-product."

Remember:

✳ *Preservatives:* Look for natural preservatives—Vitamins C and E have strong preservative qualities. Stay away from BHA, BHT, and ethoxyquin.

✳ *Fish:* Don't buy any pet food with fish in it that has a shelf life longer than six months. And watch your expiration dates!

✳ *Grains:* Look for whole grains (barley, rice, oats); no "hulls."

✳ *Fats:* Avoid anything that lists "animal fat." The fat source should be specific: beef, chicken, etc.

✳ *Carbohydrates:* Skip "beet pulp"; this is an artificial stool hardener and too high in sugar.

Finally, if you must use commercial pet food over any length of time, change brands periodically (but slowly). Many experts say that this will ensure that any nutrient deficiencies in a particular food won't have long-term effects. Also, alternate between dry food and canned. Canned food is generally better nutritionally than dry food because it contains fewer grain ingredients and fewer preservatives, and canning itself is a preservative process. Dry food can offer some minimal dental benefits for some animals for whom wet food causes problems. Find three or four foods your pet likes and alternate among them.

Table Scraps:
The Do's and Dont's

How about table scraps—human food—as a supplement to a commercial diet? In a household that primarily feeds its pets run-of-the-mill commercial pet food, table scraps may well be the *healthiest* fare the pet eats, whether a slice of ham or a few green beans from the dinner table or a handful of popcorn in the family room. Unfortunately, feeding our pets human food has fallen into disfavor, not so much for dietary reasons as for behavioral ones: a begging dog or a cat sauntering up to the gravy boat is not our idea of animal etiquette.

That is not to say that feeding your pet table scraps is sufficient as a method of providing balanced nutrition. But when you consider that much of what constitutes good nutrition for the mammalian pet is also good nutrition for the mammalian pet *owner,* you will realize that there are great opportunities right in your own kitchen that will help both parties: the pet will eat better, and the pet owner gets to economize. As for aiding and abetting a begging attitude, never feed your pet at the table (or under it). Table scraps should supplement regular food at regular feeding times in the good old bowl, but should never account for more than ten percent of what the pet eats. And don't give your pets the idea that the dining room table is their own feeding platform.

What Scraps Can I Feed My Pet?

Your dog or cat can eat most of the things a human would normally eat, but not all things. Here's a list:

Meat: Yes, but limit giving the skin of poultry. Make it a special and infrequent treat.

Chocolate: No. Chocolate contains theobromine, natural in the coca plant, harmless to humans but neurotoxic to dogs and cats in sufficient quantities. One Hershey's Kiss won't be a threat to most pets; a square of Baker's chocolate could be serious.

Onions: No. In significant quantities, onions can cause hemolytic anemia. Look for watery eyes in cat or dog as a sign that someone got into the onion sack.

Garlic: No. Although it is not particularly harmful to the pet, it is in the onion family, so excessive use is not a good idea.

Grapes and raisins: No. Animals have died from eating grapes and raisins, though no one knows why.

Bones (cooked): No. Bones are good only if raw. Cooking not only takes out many of the nutrients from the bone, but makes it dangerously splintery. A raw bone has enough moisture in it to keep it from being reduced to sharp shards that could be injurious.

Q.: **What human foods are bad for dogs?**

a.: Chocolate, onions, raisins, grapes, soy products, citrus.

Dairy products: Many milk products can cause gastric distress in dogs and cats. Fermented-type milk products, including yogurt, kefir, buttermilk, and cottage cheese, are okay, and can be an excellent source of calcium and protein. As for cheese—it's not as bad as milk, but you should avoid the processed cheeses. A little parmesan sprinkled on the pet food is a great idea; it has lots of protein per ounce (ten grams) and is very delectable to cats and dogs alike.

Myth

Introduction of healthy food will
give my pet diarrhea.

The Truth: Although a looser stool may result as you introduce healthier food to your pet, this is for two very good reasons: (1) your pet is ridding itself if old toxins during the change-over, expelling all the chemicals and preservatives that have built up; (2) healthy food does not contain the artificial stool hardeners, like beetroot and tomato pomace, that commercial foods employ to make pet owners believe their products are healthy. They are not.

Legumes and nuts: Yes. Both are good for cats and dogs in small quantities. Nuts should be ground and legumes well cooked, not raw.

Soy products: No. Pets can't utilize the amino acid complex from soy. You will find a lot of soy in commercial pet food because it is a cheap and plentiful protein source; it just happens to be useless to a dog or cat. It is not terribly harmful, but it may cause gas in some pets. A little tofu or some soy sprouts won't hurt your pet, but it won't do them much good either.

Potatoes: Yes and No. White potatoes have little or no nutritive value for a dog or a cat, but they're not harmful. Sweet potatoes are another story: they have more fiber, and the Vitamin A that makes the tubers orange is excellent. Potatoes should be well-cooked. *Do not give dogs raw potato skin peelings.*

Bacon: No. It's full of nitrates.

Pan drippings: No, not in quantity. Chicken and turkey pan drippings can lead to pancreatitis. (Drizzling a little over your pet's bowl—just a little—will do no harm. Just don't set down the pan in front of her.)

Cereal: Yes and No. No to sweetened cereals. Whole grain cold cereals are excellent, as are oats, which must be cooked. Uncooked grains can soak up too much moisture once eaten.

Fruit: Yes and No. No citrus: it's too acidic (though a little orange might be tolerated). Apples, pears, bananas, melons, peaches, and dried fruits are very good.

Bread: Yes and No. As with humans, white and refined flour breads are close to zero nutritionally, but they aren't harmful. Whole grain or seeded breads are better; they're full of excellent fiber.

Cookies: No. Sugar is not good for pets; artificial sweeteners are worse. Stay away from candies and cookies that contain sugar or artificial sweetener.

Raw vegetables: Yes, but be sure they are fresh and chopped. Some people recommend juicing; if you don't mind, go ahead. But will your pet eat it? Not all do.

Helpful Hint

Spicing or flavoring: Flavoring with a little meat broth or an herb such as ginger, may be the trigger to get your pet to enjoy vegetables.

Homemade Pet Food:
Pros and Cons

The major arguments against homemade pet food are economic, dietetic, and pragmatic. That is, it's too costly, it's not healthy enough, and it's impractical. None of these arguments can withstand scrutiny, except perhaps the last. Who am I to say what is possible or practical for any given pet owner? There are many reasons why cooking for an animal just won't work for some people: their own health, their schedule, their orientation toward cooking of any sort.

Q.: What human foods are bad for cats?

A.: Chocolate, onions, raisins, grapes, soy products, citrus.

But I can say from experience (which jibes, I believe, with common sense) that offering your dog or cat a home-made menu is not more expensive than going the commercial route if—and this is a crucial if—you are interested in feeding your pet well. Low-rent commercial dog food indifferently fed, with little concern for the dog's well-being, is no doubt easier on the pocketbook than more expensive food of any sort, whether commercial or home-prepared. But let me see your vet bills. You pay one way or the other. Or your pet does.

Q. I cook for my dog. What vitamins and minerals should I add to his diet of human-grade food?

Q. I suggest a top-quality fish oil capsule, a probiotic, and a multivitamin/mineral formulated for your pet from Standard Process (Wisconsin).

Let me stress this: *The ingredients for preparing pet food at home can be purchased cheaply.* Yes, you should get organic meat; yes, it should be free-range. Yes, you should get vegetables in season (though frozen are okay), and fresh fruit, and whole grains, and high-quality vegetable oils, and supplements from good companies. But you needn't always go top end. And aren't chicken necks and wings and thighs fairly cheap? Isn't oatmeal cheap? Aren't apples and celery cheap? Yogurt won't break the bank. I feed six adult pedigreed dogs for six weeks on about $300. That's $50 a week, dinner and breakfast and snacks—for six. For one dog, that's less than $10 a week. Think about what you spend (you commercial pet food buyers) on canned and bagged food per week. Can it be much less than this?

As for the dietetic argument, that's the one that commercial pet food companies like to hear. But in truth, it is an argument also made by the American Veterinary Medical Association. In fact, the AVMA is against all kinds of human food: "Table scraps should definitely not be a part of your pet's diet," says AVMA President Roger Mahr. "Gravies, meat fats and poultry skin can readily cause stomach and intestinal upsets, and even lead to a life-threatening condition called pancreatitis in dogs. Bones will splinter when chewed and cannot be digested by the animal's system. Chocolate can be poisonous to them, but it tastes good so pets will eat it if they have the opportunity. Dark chocolate used in baking is particularly dangerous to pets, and xylitol—a common sweetener in baked goods—has been linked with liver failure and death in dogs."

To which I say to my readers, as I did above: Be intelligent. Don't feed them chicken skin and fat drippings and chocolate and cooked bones.

Q.· My dog is a fussy eater and is on prescription dry food for his sensitive stomach. I often mix a little bit of peanut butter or plain yogurt into his food to make it more appealing to him. Is this safe?

a.· Peanut butter is hard to digest, and unless it's organic with no salt or sugar added, I would avoid it completely. A full-fat plain yogurt is a great addition.

The AVMA also contends that pet nutrition is so vastly complicated and implies that the commercial pet food industry is so on top of these complicated issues that an intelligent person cooking at home can't possibly match what's in the can, pouch, or bag from the supermarket. To which I say: Get thee to a rendering plant.

The AVMA's advice—no table scraps, no homemade food—makes sense only if a pet owner cares to know nothing about what his or her pet needs. A diet of indiscriminately offered human food is no good, and could be worse than commercial pet food. But the point of this book is to educate the pet owner so his or her efforts in the home kitchen are more than a match for the heavily processed commercial food, which is prepared with shelf life and profit margins in mind.

Tips on Feeding the Homemade Diet

Cook the meat. I am against raw food in general, because of some complications that I will get to in a subsequent section. The risk of bacterial infection is too high, and the consequences too dire, not to cook meat. However, small bony portions of chicken, for example, can be quickly submerged in boiling water to kill any possible skin bacteria but without cooking the bones excessively.

Grains should be cooked. Uncooked grains can swell in the pet's stomach, and can also be passed without yielding nutritional benefit.

Vegetables should be steamed or served raw. Always chop or slice vegetables or run them through a food processor.

Oils should be refrigerated. This is especially true of safflower, sunflower, olive, and the more expensive flaxseed and sesame oils. A teaspoon of oil atop the pet food serving will help maintain a lustrous coat and clear skin.

Fruit should be chopped. Apples, pears, watermelon, and berries are all good for your pet and rich in vitamins.

Why Raw Food Diets Failed

et's look at why raw food diets for pets caught on for a while.

First, cats and dogs were once avid predators. Several thousand years ago, they ate all their meals raw, and certainly as recently as a hundred years ago they ate raw prey to a considerable extent. So raw food is not anathema to a dog's or a cat's instincts, taste buds, or digestive system.

Second, a study by Frances Pottenger, in which cats were fed a diet of raw meat and bone, cod liver oil, and raw milk, had no significant health problems through three successive generations, compared to three variant control diets involving cooked meat, pasteurized milk, and even sweetened condensed milk. The control group, on the other hand, experienced a host of health and reproductive problems. The study lasted 10 years and involved 900 cats. Pottenger (1909–1967) was a California M.D. whose principal research involved tuberculosis; his original observations about pet diet stemmed from TB experiments he was running on cats. "Pottenger's cats" are cited often in the raw food community as a scientific basis for the wisdom of feeding only raw food.

Third, raw food is good for pets, relatively speaking. Compared to much of the commercial pet food available, it offers something processed food delivers poorly: bioavailable nutrients and crucial enzymes that are killed by rendering and drying.

Now, let's look at why raw food diets failed.

In the main, I attribute the decline in the popularity of the raw food diet to the strictness of its regimen, the zealotry of its promotion, and the *ick* factor.

For example, raw food diet enthusiasts insist that the intricacies of its execution must be exactingly followed. Consider these instructions, from a typical pro-raw website, on determining serving size:

Multiply your dog's weight by 16 to get the number of ounces he weighs.

Multiply that by .02, which gives you 2% of his body weight.

Multiply that by .6 to give you the weight of RMB you should feed. That is, chicken necks, wings, backs etc.

Go back to the 2% of his body weight again and multiply that number by .4 to get the weight in ounces of vegetable patty mix you should feed.

The raw food diet also discourages feeding any grains, discourages "contamination" by snack or kibble; and requires extra digestive enzymes to help the pet process the raw food.

As for zeal, the raw food folks are a bit much. So keen are they on the concept "raw" that they will even accept a total vegetarian diet (puréed raw veggies), which shows, in my view, a reckless disregard for what cats and dogs need: animal protein and animal-source vitamins and minerals.

The *ick* factor comes in when you find yourself handling pounds and pounds of raw chicken and beef and grinding the offal—organ meat, such as liver, kidney, heart—into "veggie patties." There is also the unfortunate period of adjustment that any pet would have to make to raw food, filled with gastric distress requiring uncomfortable spells of enforced fasting. And let's not get into the fecal lowlights of said transition. The nickname for the raw food diet is BARF: bones and raw food. The name tells you a lot.

As I have already indicated, and will reiterate, I do not recommend anything close to a raw food diet. Yes to raw bones, a must; yes to occasional bits of raw meat and very lightly cooked chicken. But cooked grain is an essential component, as are vegetables, raw and lightly cooked (carrots are healthier when cooked). In addition (without being an alarmist, which I am not), a steady diet of raw meat and bone seems to improve the slim chances of salmonella or trichinosis invading your pet's system. Why flirt with that?

Mixing Commercial Food with Table Scraps and Homemade Cookin'

If you find it more convenient to have commercial pet food as part of your pet's diet, by all means do so. If you can't bring yourself to deny your pet some food from the table, don't feel guilty—just give him the good stuff and not the bad. But I strongly recommend that you prepare the bulk of your pet's diet yourself. It is safe, nutritious, and inexpensive. And it can be fun.

Acceptable Commercial Foods

In my experience, there are two pet food companies whose products for cats and dogs I recommend as a component of a mixed-source diet: Flint River Ranch, out of Roswell, Georgia, and Nature's Logic, of Lincoln, Nebraska. Neither of these companies, I might add, were cited in the extensive recall of this spring.

Flint River double-bakes its pet food, which, unlike the high-heat steam process used by most other commercial pet food operators, keeps in many of the basic nutrients while making other nutrients—especially in the grains—more bioavailable. Flint also uses human-grade meats. They make food canned and dry, for both cats and dogs.

Nature's Logic also stacks up well and offers such complex and varied animal sources as rabbit, duck, and salmon, in addition to beef and chicken.

Each of these companies avoids chemical preservatives, and Nature's Logic also avoids using any chemically synthesized vitamins or minerals. Although both are more expensive than most other commercial pet foods, for my dollar this is the way to go if you must have some ready-made food to supplement your home-cooked diet and to take with you on the road with your pets.

The Table Scraps

When you are cleaning up after your own dinner, think like your cat or dog for a moment. Take a look at what's left over and consider if a portion of that might not only be a delectable treat for the furry one, but something that will add to his nutritional roster of things he needs. Uneaten cubes of squash, a bit of the roast, a heel of the whole wheat baguette, the slab of uneaten fried egg—these things, your pet would like you to know, would look great in that very special bowl on the floor.

The mother lode of the diet, of course, is what you make yourself. In Part Three of this book I hope to help you with that by providing easy recipes and dollops of encouragement.

part three

Home Cooking Recipes

Know Your Breed

efore I get to the home-prep recipes I recommend, it is important for you to take a moment to consider just what kind of dog or cat you have. This will help you hone your instincts as to what makes sense for your pet.

The breed of your dog or cat can tell you a lot about its needs. It can tell you what diet, climate, and kinds of activities it is accustomed to. It may tell you what behavioral attributes you can expect to be foregrounded in its manner; it can tell you how long you might expect it to live, what kinds of diseases or maladies it might be prone to; it might tell you what you should do and should not do, feed and not feed.

For Dogs

The American Kennel Club divides breeds into seven groups:

Herding

Working

Sporting

Non-sporting

Terriers

Toys

Hounds

Although generalizing is, by definition, an inexact science, these AKC groupings are based on a lot of wisdom.

These groups are not organized by incidental dog attributes, say, size or shape or color or length of hair. Their organization is based on the dogs' origins and breeding histories, which are very much tied up in what kinds of life these animals are not only used to, but built for. It is good to familiarize yourself with these divisions, though, as you will see, when it comes to drawing inferences relevant to feeding, there is a second, somewhat more useful way to organize the canine world.

Fun Facts

Cats have 244 bones.

Dogs have 319 bones.

Humans have 206 bones.

Now you know why pets need calcium.

The Herding Group

These wonderful doggies, until about twenty years ago, were part of the AKC Working group. They are basically the collies, sheepdogs, and shepherding animals. They are very intelligent and responsive to training. For the most part, these breeds originated in northern Europe, mostly the British Isles. They were raised on farms that had livestock. Their diets, like any dog's, requires a lot of animal protein. But because of their long hair (think collie) or thick fur (think German shepherd), they also require, and benefit from, plenty of high-quality fats.

The Working Group

These are the very strong and physical dogs, bred to perform such jobs as guarding property and pulling sleds. Akitas, malamutes, Great Danes, Bernese mountain dogs, boxers, bullmastiffs, Doberman pinschers, and rottweilers are some of the dogs in this group (as is that first dog I saw so long ago, my Great Pyrenees!). You can bet that these dogs were well fed, since, as working animals, their energy and strength was essential to their function. Sources of high protein like kidney and liver and sources of iron and calcium like raw bone and green vegetables would be central to their diet.

The Sporting Group

This companionable set of dogs, if working at all, was probably involved in either a human leisure activity or a less taxing job assignment. The group includes retrievers, spaniels, setters, pointers, and the Weimaraner. These dogs would be less accustomed to diets high in animal protein and would have a lower calorie requirement. Grains would be an essential part of their diet—or should be—though, to the extent that they are not being pushed extremely hard physically, one should be careful not to overload with carbohydrates, else the animals get fat.

The Non-sporting Group

Think puffy, cute, pretty, small, alert, active, fierce, muscular. Sound confusing? The Non-sporting group is very diverse—and this is where you begin to see how the AKC grouping falters in its applicability to our concerns about what to feed. Everything from the American Eskimo dog to the Lhasa apso is in this category, which also includes some spaniels (Tibetan), some terriers (also Tibetan), the poodle, the dalmatian, bulldogs, and spitzes. The variations in coat, size, personality, and origins make this group difficult to project dietetically.

The Terrier Group

This is a much more distinctive and unique group, with wiry coats, smallish in size (except the Airedale), self-possessed in spirit. The group includes many familiar breeds: Norwich, Kerry blue, Norfolk, Scottish, and cairn. And, of course, that dearest to me: the Bedlington. The terriers' intelligence makes them quite engaged with humans. Ancestrally, almost all terriers were what I call "ratters"—they hunted vermin. You will see the dietary implications below.

The Toy Group

The toys, as the name suggests, are small and fun. According to the American Kennel Club, the function of this group is "to embody sheer delight." You may wonder about that if a Chihuahua gets irked, but toys have been bred for nothing other than their conveniently-sized packages of companion-ability—whether Pekinese, Pomeranian, pug, poodle (again, across groups), shih tzu, or the Italian greyhound. These are delicate dogs, far removed from work or hunting. Their hyperactivity keeps them quite calorie hungry, but because of their size, their dietary needs are about the same as a cat's.

The Hound Group

These dogs hunt by sight or sound. They can make a lot of noise; they generally have good stamina, sleek coats, and a lot of strength. They range from the well-known beagle, dachshund (its own group, by the way, in Europe), and bloodhound, to the more exotic Afghan hounds, Scottish deerhounds, and salukis. These dogs are used to a lot of activity outdoors, and they thrill to the sights and smells of certain prey. These are meat eaters and bone eaters. Not that you'd forget.

The Pet Food Nation Way

As helpful as the AKC designations are in separating dogs by type, you may note that certain breeds might appear in different groups; the poodle, for example, is in both the Toy and the Non-sporting group; spaniels can be found in the Sporting as well as the Toy group. A more helpful organization is the following. This is how I see the landscape of dog breeds:

Hunting dogs
Northern working dogs
Toys
Sight hounds
Mountain dogs
Herding dogs
Working dogs
Dachshunds
Other hounds

Fun Facts

A Dog's Life

A dog's heart rate ranges from 70 to 110 beats per minute.

Breaths per minute: 10 to 30 (panting).

Average body temperature: 101.5 (same as a cat's).

Hunting dogs include Labradors, retrievers, and standard poodles (yes, they were originally hunters), along with some working water dogs, such as Newfoundlands, water spaniels, and the Portuguese water dog. They traditionally ate chicken, trout, salmon, duck and other water fowl, and geese. Occasionally they had oats or barley and predominantly ate potatoes and green beans as their vegetables. Apples would be their most likely fruit.

Northern working dogs are huskies, malamutes, and Samoyeds. They ate mostly fish, salmon, and sardines and occasionally elk, venison, and buffalo. They would likely have eaten potatoes but probably no grains.

Toys or other small companion dogs and Tibetan breeds ate fish and chicken, some lamb, plus local vegetables and brown rice, possibly millet.

Sight hounds—greyhounds, Afghans, wolfhounds, salukis, and deerhounds—all ate rabbit, venison, and poultry as well as local vegetables, including potatoes. Apples were a likely fruit; brown rice, whole barley, oats, and bulgur wheat would have been the grain sources.

Mountain dogs—rottweilers and northern district terriers (West Highland, Scottish)—ate lamb, chicken, and rabbit with wild parsley, carrots, and potatoes, as well as oats and barley.

Herding breeds like collies, shelties, corgies, and lowland (or Lake District) terriers ate cod, salmon, halibut, some lamb, and chicken. Peas and carrots were the common vegetable, along with potatoes. Oats and barley would have been their mainstay grains.

Working dogs such as German shepherds, Dobermans, schnauzers, Great Danes, Old English sheepdogs, and borzoi hounds ate beef and lamb, cabbage, and greens with oats and barley.

Dachshunds' diet was similar to the lowland terriers'. This group includes Airedales, Staffordshires, Yorkshires, and Norfolks.

Other hounds—beagles, foxhounds, and bassets—ate lamb, chicken, and rabbit with parsley, carrots, and potatoes as well as oats and barley.

As for mixed breeds, your guess is as good as mine—probably better than mine, if you own one. If you do have a mutt of mixed breed, try to determine what the predominant breed is. You can count on one thing: it probably has the best traits of all its mixed ancestors and is probably more adaptable, dietwise, then its pure-bred brethren.

For Cats

a member of our good old *Felis sylvestris catus* species, today's domesticated cat is born with a predisposition to develop bonds with humans. But as cat lovers (and haters) know, the cat is an independent force—temperamentally, of course, but its independence runs even more deeply. A domesticated cat can return to a feral, semi-wild state and not only survive there, but even reproduce.

The cat's dietary system works in high gear all of the time; it has stringent dietary requirements. Unlike dogs and humans, cats cannot turn off enzymes. They are in a constant state of glucogenesis. Felines cannot survive on a vegetarian diet, and they get almost all their water from food. It is hard to get a cat to drink.

Cats function at a high metabolic rate, so their need for protein is great. A grain-based diet, as our commercial pet foods generally are, presents a real challenge to the cat. Cats need taurine (available only from meat protein), arachidonic acid (found only in animal tissue), and preformed Vitamin A.

Fun Facts

What's that purring sound?
A cat's normal body temperature in 101.5.
Heart rate is 110 to 180 beats per minute.
Respiratory rate is 30 to 50 breaths a minute,
nearly 4 times the rate of humans.

Although cats were long ago kept for utilitarian purposes as vermin control, they have since overwhelmingly been bred for their companionability and appearance—that is, their color and markings. Cats today break down into four classes, which are hard to classify as to actual geographic origin. This is because, as principal rat catchers, cats were often aboard ships that stopped at many ports around the world.

Short-haired breeds

Long-haired breeds

Rex

Spotted

Short-Haired Breeds

This group includes the Abyssinians, the Siamese and Oriental shorthairs, the tailless Manx cats, and the British, European, and American shorthairs, which are basically your common cat. A "domestic short-haired cat" has no pedigree.

Long-Haired Breeds

The long-haired cats include the Maine Coon cat, Persian cats, and the Angora, among many others. The Persian is probably the oldest of these, and is the most popular pedigreed cat in the United States. It is docile, gentle, and relatively inactive. It should be fed carefully, and fats and carbohydrates should be kept to a minimum. The Maine Coon cat is the second most popular longhair in the United States. It is a large cat, with long legs and a soft, profuse coat and is very hardy, athletic, playful, and amiable.

Rex

These are the cats that some believe came from somewhere else—like outer space. Actually, they come from two places in England, Cornwall and Devon. They have a distinct, pixie-like head, and their coats are mostly downlike.

Spotted Cats

These cats are most often the result of elaborate breeding. Consider the ocicat, a spotted cat that resulted from the interbreeding of Abyssinian, Siamese, and American shorthair. It is the only spotted domestic breed selectively bred to emulate the look of the cats of the wild: a big, active animal with an athletic appearance. It is well-muscled, and its satiny fur shows off both its muscles and its ocelot-like spots to great effect. Spotted cats can be the ultimate in finicky, which means: give them what they want—they're beautiful.

The domestication of the cat has been so short (4,000 years) compared to the dog (perhaps 15,000 years), that cats, regardless of type—whether longhair, shorthair, rex, or spotted—pretty much eat the same thing. Come back to me in 11,000 years and there may be more variation, but right now, you feed a Manx much like you'd feed a Maine Coon. And the same for everything in between.

Basic Recipes for Dogs

These are my basic recipes for a typical dog, a twenty-pound dog. If feeding a forty-pound dog, double the ingredients for their daily ration. If feeding twice daily, split the ration in half. These generic recipes will provide your dog with twenty-five to forty percent fat and meat protein.

A couple of notes: I like to do my light sautéing of the animal protein—whether chicken, turkey, or hamburger—as well as some of the veggies on occasion, in organic coconut oil. It has no trans fats, even when used for frying.

I also recommend that you have a good probiotic on hand as a supplement. There are several good ones on the market.

The probiotic helps balance the healthy bacteria in the gut of both dogs and cats.

Remember to provide plenty of clean drinking water— as much as your dog needs.

I recommend digestive enzymes ("green food"), and a multivitamin mineral specifically for your pets several times weekly.

Happy cooking!

Cooking Ahead:

A Bulk Recipe for Dogs

2 Tbsp. oil (organic oils: olive, coconut, safflower, fish oil or codliver oil)

¾ cup water or low-sodium broth

1½ cup puréed chopped or lightly steamed vegetables

1 cup well-cooked grains (oatmeal, barley, rice, millet, quinoa, or buckwheat)

1 lb. raw meat, poultry, or cooked fish (salmon, mackerel, whiting, cod, sardines)

Mix thoroughly and freeze in daily portions (2 to 3 cups for 20-pound dog). Thaw and warm before serving (do not microwave). Feel free to top with sprinkling of high-quality kibble or 1 Tbsp. of full-fat yogurt. Cooked organ meat (¼ cup) can be added several times a week.

Dog Breakfast:

Monday–Friday

⅛ to ¼ cup mixture of organic chicken hearts, gizzards, livers

¾ cup string beans, either fresh or frozen

¼ cup grated zucchini

small handful chopped romaine lettuce

heaping tsp. organic full-fat yogurt

⅛ tsp. probiotic liquid

1 fish oil capsule

Very briefly sauté meat in 1 Tbsp. organic coconut oil just to warm, not to cook. Then add all vegetables and lightly sauté till their color brightens. Place in dog bowl, top with fish oil capsule, probiotic, and yogurt.

Dog's Weekend Breakfast

Use a duck egg or other organic chicken egg instead of
meat twice a week.

¼ cup grain (brown rice or sweet potato or pasta,
oatmeal, or quinoa)

½ cup string beans

Dog's Every Night Dinner

½ cup boiled chicken,* which can include the chicken fat

1 cup lightly steamed vegetables: cauliflower, broccoli,
cabbage, bok choy. You can add tomatoes or pumpkin
as well.

* Feel free to substitute cooked ostrich, buffalo, or lamb.

Dog Snack/Lunch

A dog should be fed only twice a day. But I do indulge my
dogs in a healthy dog biscuit at night, and if they are particularly active (and insistent), I have raw organic chicken neck
handy for lunch. Dip the chicken neck in boiling water for
just a few seconds.

Rice and Beans

½ cup cooked brown rice

½ cup lightly cooked hamburger

½ cup well-cooked kidney beans

fish oil capsule

½ tsp. calcium powder (eggshell powder; see sidebar for
   preparation)

multivitamin/mineral for dogs

Makes 2 servings (20-pound dog)

You can substitute turkey or chicken for the hamburger; instead of brown rice, you can substitute cooked barley, bulgur, millet, or oats.

Fish and Oats

3 cups cooked oatmeal

1 cup fish (mackerel, salmon, whiting, sardine—canned
   salmon or sardines are okay)

1 cup of green beans

½ tsp. eggshell powder

Makes 2 servings (20-pound dog)

Mainly Vegetable

1½ cups cooked bulgur or whole wheat couscous

⅔ cup chicken, fish, hamburger, or turkey

½ tsp. eggshell powder or ½ cup lightly steamed green
   leafy vegetable

1 cup grated zucchini (raw) or cooked cauliflower or
   broccoli

Makes 2 servings (20-pound dog)

Lite Dinner: Beef and Lentils

1 cup boiled lentils

1 cup cooked rice

2 tsp. oil

½ cup lightly cooked hamburger

pinch of sea salt

½ tsp. eggshell powder

multivitamin/mineral supplement

Makes 2 servings (20-pound dog)

Eggshell Powder: Great Calcium Supplement

This is ideal for a calcium boost.

Wash and dry a dozen empty eggshells and bake at 300 degrees for 10 minutes. Grind into a power in mortar or coffee grinder. Mix ¼ tsp. into your dog's or cat's food several times a week. (If using organic eggs, no need to bake.)

Doggie's Sunday Fare

1½ cups cooked pasta

⅓ cup cooked millet

1 cup roasted chicken (including skin as special treat)

1 cup pureed peas and carrots

¼ cup lightly steamed carrots

multivitamin/mineral supplement

½ tsp. eggshell powder

Makes 2 servings (20-pound dog)

Dogs with Kidney Disease

Always, without exception, use the best quality protein sources for a pet with kidney trouble. I offer two recipes.

Note: daily ration (2 servings) for 20-pound dog

Meat and Potatoes

¼ cup lean hamburger or chicken (cooked)

3 cups cooked potato with skin

1 Tbsp. chicken fat oil

pinch of sea salt

500 mg Vitamin C (Ester-C is best)

1 Tbsp. minced parsley

½ tsp. eggshell powder

multivitamin/mineral supplement

Note: if kidney stones are suspected, cut the Vitamin C dosage in half.

Eggs and Potatoes

1 egg (scrambled, or hard-boiled and chopped)

3 cups boiled potato with skin

1 Tbsp. chicken fat or fish oil capsule

½ tsp. eggshell powder

pinch of sea salt

500 mg Vitamin C (Ester-C is best)

1 Tbsp. minced parsley

multivitamin/mineral supplement

Note: if kidney stones are suspected, cut the Vitamin C dosage in half.

Canine Heart Diet

¾ cup lean beef, chicken, or fish (well-cooked)

3 cups boiled potatoes with skins

2 tsp. chicken fat

1 fish oil capsul

½ tsp. eggshell powder

multivitamin/mineral supplement

So, What's with the Chicken Fat?

Cats and dogs, unless they have a severe thyroid problem, aren't prone to high cholesterol. It is perfectly fine to set aside the fat from your family's chicken and refrigerate it or cook it up lightly. Add 1 to 2 teaspoons to your pet's food.

Dogs with Cancer

Canine Cancer Care

Tumor cells rely heavily upon carbohydrates for their energy, but those cells cannot utilize fats for energy, while the rest of the body can. As such, diets with increased fat content may slow tumor growth.

1 cup lightly cooked meat with fat

1½ cup mixed vegetables

2 Tbsp. salmon oil

½ tsp. eggshell powder

a pinch of sea salt

multivitamin/mineral supplement

Makes 2 servings (20-pound dog)

Basic Recipes for Cats

*A*s we know, cats need protein. I recommend that 75 percent (by weight) of their diet come from animal-protein source. The recipes below are for a 10-pound cat. Notice that, for cats, I go lighter on the grains (you may leave them out completely).

Cooking Ahead:

A Bulk Recipe for Cats

This recipe is for cooking a batch of high-nutrition food, which you can divide into single servings and freeze. When preparing to serve, do not microwave; rather, slowly warm ever so slightly on the stove.

2 Tbsp. oil (organic oils: olive, coconut, safflower, or fish oil)

¾ cup water or low-sodium broth

¼ cup well-cooked grains (oatmeal, barley, rice, millet, quinoa, or buckwheat)

¼ cup puréed raw or lightly steamed puréed vegetable (raw: zucchini, squash, broccoli, green beans; cooked: carrots, winter squash, pumpkin, yams/sweet potatoes)

1 lb. raw meat (ground turkey, chicken, lamb, buffalo, ostrich, venison)

or

1 lb. cooked fish (mackerel, salmon, whiting, cod, tuna or sardines)

Mix thoroughly and freeze in daily portions (½ cup for 10-pound cat). Thaw and warm before serving (do not microwave). Cooked organ meat (¼ cup) can be added several times a week. Hint: Keep a dish of fresh wheat grass handy for snacks. Add ⅛ tsp. eggshell powder daily and a feline vitamin/mineral supplement several times a week. A probiotic and enzyme powder are recommended.

Cat's Breakfast for a

10-Pound Cat

¼ cup yogurt, kefir, buttermilk, or cottage cheese

¼ cup chicken heart, liver, kidney (cooked)

1 fish oil capsule

1 Tbsp. puréed pumpkin (canned whole pumpkin is
okay)

1 tsp. parsley, romaine, or spinach, chopped

For the pumpkin you may substitute puréed carrots, wheat grass, chopped string beans, cucumbers, zucchini, squash, or corn.

Note: Don't serve liver more than twice a week.

Cat's Dinner for a

10-Pound Cat

¼ cup very lightly sautéed or boiled chicken or fish

1 tsp. greens (wheat grass, collards, spinach, parsley,
etc.)

1 Tbsp. cooked potatoes, turnip, parsnip

Note: Add ¼ tsp. of eggshell powder several times a week for calcium boost.

Cat's Special Breakfast for 10-Pound Cat

⅛ cup cottage cheese

1 egg, lightly scrambled

⅛ cup well-cooked oatmeal

⅛ cup puréed string bean

pinch of sea salt

Helpful Hint

Nuts for Cats and Dogs: Ground nuts are an excellent source of fatty acids. Pets love the taste.

Use organic unroasted, unsalted nuts—walnuts and almonds are best, but peanuts are also fine. Be sure to grind them or reduce to a paste. But no peanut butter unless no salt or sugar added.

Holiday Dinner for Cats

¼ cup cooked polenta or cornmeal

1 tsp. vegetable oil or salmon oil

½ cup ground turkey or chicken (cooked)

1 tsp. fresh vegetable purée

multivitamin/mineral supplement

⅛ tsp. eggshell powder

Makes 2 servings (10-pound cat)

Cat's Mixed Grill and Pasta

⅛ cup cooked chicken

⅛ cup cooked whole wheat pasta

2 sardines

⅛ cup lightly steamed vegetable

multivitamin/mineral supplement

Makes 2 servings (10-pound cat)

Some Rules of Thumb for Cats and Dogs

* *Lean meats:* turkey, liver, mackerel, chicken, tuna, heart
* *Fatty meats:* roaster chicken, lamb, hamburger
* *High-protein grains:* buckwheat, barley, bulgur, millet
* *Lower protein grains:* brown rice, corn meal, rolled oats
* *High-protein legumes:* red kidney beans, lentils, split peas, white or black beans (soak and cook well)
* *Careful:* Spinach, chard, and rhubarb are high in oxalic acid, which interferes with calcium absorption.
* *Fruits and berries:* all good, except grapes and raisins

Helpful Hint

Natural Digestive Enzymes: Herbs and grasses (parsley, romaine, wheat grass, etc.) contain enzymes to aid in the digestion. A must.

Cat's Hardy Meal

4 oz. canned tuna fish, salmon, tuna, mackerel

1 hard-boiled egg (chopped)

1 fish oil capsule

⅛ cup puréed vegetable

multivitamin/mineral supplement

Makes 2 servings (10-pound cat)

For Cats with Kidney Disease

A relatively low-protein diet may help reduce clinical signs of uremic toxins in the presence of renal dysfunction. Vitamin C helps flush the kidneys. If kidney stones are suspected, cut the Vitamin C dosage in half.

For Kidney Care I

¼ cup cooked chicken or other lean meat

½ oz. canned clams

½ cup cooked white rice

1 Tbsp. chicken fat

pinch of sea salt

¼ tsp. eggshell powder

500 mg Vitamin C (Ester-C is best)

¼ tsp. parsley

For Kidney Care II

3 egg whites, hard-boiled (chopped)

1 oz. canned sardines

½ cup cooked rice

1 Tbsp. chicken fat

pinch of sea salt

⅓ tsp. eggshell powder

⅛ tsp. parsley

500 mg Vitamin C (Ester-C is best)

multivitamin/mineral supplement

For Feline Heart Care

¾ cup cooked chicken

or

½ cup tuna, mackerel, or salmon (cooked)

1 oz. canned chopped clams

2 tsp. chicken fat or salmon oil

¼ tsp. calcium powder

multivitamin/mineral supplement

For Feline Cancer Care

¾ cup lightly cooked meat with fat

1 Tbsp. puréed mixed vegetables

2 tsp. salmon oil

¼ tsp. eggshell powder

multivitamin/mineral supplement

Special Diets for Sick Pets

✳ *Arthritis:* Avoid all nightshade vegetables (peppers, eggplant, potato, tomato).

✳ *Kidney or bladder stones:* Avoid spinach, asparagus, dairy products, organ meats, legumes, parsley, carrots, kale, potatoes, cucumbers. No grains.

✳ *Diabetes:* Serve three meals daily. Avoid fatty meats. Introduce some raw foods, as it stimulates the pancreas. Add dandelion, garlic, parsley. Feed grains.

✳ *Diarrhea:* Limit water; liquid should come from broth of meat bones, well-cooked rice, canned pumpkin.

Joan's Vitamin Chart

*N*ature makes vitamins in complete food forms. We use them as a whole, not as isolated pieces. Whole food nutrients are by and large the most usable (bioavailable) and bioactive in the body. These nutrients work together synergistically to achieve maximum biological effect. This chart shows you the essential vitamins your dog and cat need, along with their sources, their function, the signs of a deficiency in that vitamin, and the signs of an excess. This is for your general information.

You should purchase a general multivitamin to give your dog or cat. This chart will help you understand the why and the wherefore of the vitamins you are providing. It will also let you know, via the natural food sources for each, which vitamins you are providing in your pet food.

Nutrient & Source	Function	Deficiency	Excess
BIOTIN liver, kidney, egg yolk, yeast, milk, legumes	metabolize fat, protein, and vitamin C	skin lesions, anemia, hair loss, muscle weakness, heart disease	nontoxic
FOLIC ACID liver, kidney, yeast, leafy green vegetables	formation of red blood cells, builds antibodies, cell division	anemia, birth defects, poor appetite	nontoxic
CHOLINE organ meats, fish, egg yolk, yeast, wheat germ, dairy, legumes, whole grains	fat emulsifier, nerve function and structure	fatty liver, neurological disorders, heart disease, thymus degeneration	diarrhea
VITAMIN A fish oil, liver, eggs, dairy, dark green and yellow vegetables	skeletal growth, epithelial tissue, immune system, reproduction, vision, nerve function	skeletal deformities, cleft palate, skin lesions, night-hyperactivity, liver damage, blindness, infection, deafness	liver problems
VITAMIN B1 (thiamine) whole grains, meat, legumes, nuts, yeast	digestion of carbs and protein	stool eating, anorexia, muscle weakness, CNS disturbances	nontoxic
VITAMIN B2 (riboflavin) mill products, organ meat, eggs, green vegetables	digestion of carbs and fats, cell growth	skin lesions, neurological disorders, shedding/oily coat	nontoxic

Nutrient & Source	Function	Deficiency	Excess
VITAMIN B3 (niacin) liver, meat, eggs, dairy, whole grain, legumes	stimulates circulation, processes amino acids, carbs, and glucose, utilization of fatty acids, aids HCL production	dermatitis, diarrhea, dementia	nontoxic
VITAMIN B5 (pantothenic acid) liver, kidney, dairy, yeast, legumes, wheat germ, peanuts	fatty acid synthesis, steroid production, reduces stress	premature graying, low blood sugar, Addison's disease, anorexia, reduced immunity	none observed
VITAMIN B6 (pyridoxine) liver, meat, yeast, dairy, whole grains, egg yolk, fish	metabolism of protein & amino acids, electrolyte balance, red-blood cell production (note: destroyed by heat)	neurological disorders, anemia, heart disease, tooth decay, dermatitis, swollen tongue, pregnancy disorder, lowered immunity	none observed
VITAMIN B12 liver, kidney, meat, fish, poultry, eggs	formation of red blood cells, aids assimilation of fats, carbs, proteins	anemia, impaired neurological function, fatigue	nontoxic

Nutrient & Source	Function	Deficiency	Excess
VITAMIN C (ascorbic acid) citrus, green vegetables, berries, tomatoes	formation of collagen, capillary integrity	weak bones, dental problems	nontoxic
VITAMIN D (fat-soluble) fish liver oils, yeast, egg yolk, sunlight	calcium & phosphorus absorption, bone growth, regulation of calcium	defective bone growth (rickets)	hyper-calcemia
VITAMIN E (tocopherol, fat-soluble) nuts, brown rice, wheat germ, green leafy vegetables, safflower oil, whole grains, soybean, sunflower oil	antioxidant, enhances immune system, aids healing, prevents scars, retards aging, increases sperm production	reproductive failure, muscle deformation, weakened immunity, heart disease, parasitis in cats	nontoxic
VITAMIN K (fat-soluble) liver, green leafy vegetables	essential to blood clotting, protein production	internal bleeding	anemia
VITAMIN F vegetable oils: safflower, sunflower, wheat germ oil, linseed	healthy skin and hair	skin conditions, poor coat	none observed

Know Your Minerals

inerals are essential for bone formation, muscle metabolism, fluid balance, and nervous system function. Our pets ingest minerals from water and food: meat, grain, vegetables, fruit, legumes. Minerals depend on each other as well as on the presence of other nutrients in order to function; conversely, the presence of some vitamins can inhibit the absorption or metabolizing of some minerals.

All minerals are absorbed in the gastrointestinal tract and eliminated through the kidneys as urine or processed and broken down by the liver or by digestive secretions. Minerals that remain—that are stored in the body—will be in bone or muscle.

The macro-minerals include calcium, phosphorous, magnesium, and sulfur, plus the electrolytes sodium, potassium, and chloride. Micro—or trace minerals needed in minute amounts are iron, boron, chromium, copper, fluoride, iodine, molybdenum, silicon, manganese, selenium, and zinc.

Beware: Trying to supplement individual trace elements is risky, as a pinch goes a long way. Too much becomes quickly toxic.

Major (Macro) Minerals

Calcium and **phosphorus** are necessary in a specific ratio for teeth and bone formation, storage and transfer of energy, and nerve and muscle function. An imbalance in the ratio will cause skeletal problems.

Sources: Green leafy vegetables, sardines, blackstrap molasses, salmon, nuts (calcium). Fish, meat (muscle and organ), beans, poultry (phosphorus).

Potassium and **sodium** work in tandem, maintaining fluid balance in cells for proper muscle and nerve function. Sodium deficiency is unlikely in our pets, but potassium deficiency causes muscle weakness and heart and kidney lesions. Also hypertension.

Sources: Meats, poultry, fish, bananas, whole grains, sweet potato, squash, beans, dried apricots. Sodium chloride is found everywhere in the diet as "salt." Salt-induced hypertension in the dog or cat is not usually seen.

Fun Facts

Front-loaded: On average, dogs carry 75 percent of their weight from the shoulders forward. Cats carry 75 percent of their weight from their hips backward.

Magnesium is found in soft tissue and bone; it interacts with calcium to provide proper muscle and nerve function and aids in the body's use of potassium and sodium. Deficiency leads to muscle weakness and sometimes convulsions. Excessive amounts in a cat lead to lower urinary tract blockages.

Sources: Whole grains, green leafy vegetables, meat, beans, bananas, apricots.

Sulfur is found everywhere in the body and is most highly concentrated in skin, nails, and hair. It is used for wound healing and synthesis of chondroitin-sulfate. It is easily destroyed by antibiotics killing bacteria in the intestines. Sulfur supplemented as MSM (methyl sulfonyl methane) will help with skin conditions and arthritis.

Sources: Meat, fish, dairy products, eggs.

Trace (Micro) Minerals

Trace elements are iron, copper, zinc, manganese, iodine, selenium, cobalt, boron, chromium, iodine, molybdenum, and silicon. Although dietary requirements are minimal, they are essential to general good health.

Herbs and Their Uses

* *Aloe vera:* arthritis, digestion.
* *Chamomile:* indigestion, calmative.
* *Dandelion:* arthritis, liver function (hepatitis).
* *Ginger:* circulation, digestion.
* *Kelp / seaweed:* tonic for stomach, improves pigmentation.
* *Milk thistle:* liver tonic.
* *Mint:* digestion.
* *Mullein:* nerve tonic.
* *Nettle tea infusion:* relieves itchy dander.
* *Slippery elm bark:* relieves diarrhea.
* *Valerian root:* calmative.
* *Yucca:* arthritis.

Iron is critical for healthy red blood cells and an essential component of enzymes involved in cellular respiration. Iron from animal sources appears to be more readily absorbed than that from vegetable sources. There is some evidence that feeds high in soy products could interfere with iron absorption, leading to a recommendation that soy-based foods be supplemented with an iron supplement at a dosage higher than normally required.

Sources: Beef, liver, beans.

Copper is necessary in the production of melanin, the pigment that colors coat and skin, and is linked to iron metabolism. Deficiencies can cause impaired bone growth and anemia, even if iron intake is normal.

Sources: Whole wheat, beef liver, nuts, seeds, shellfish.

Zinc is heavily involved in skin and coat health, enzyme function, and protein digestion. Deficiencies lead to poor growth, reproductive failure, and skin lesions.

Sources: Lamb, pork, liver, eggs, wheat germ, beans.

Manganese is necessary for collagen formation and lipid metabolism, as well as normal reproduction. Deficiencies include reproductive failure and impaired growth.

Sources: Whole grains, nuts, peas, beets, green leafy vegetables, eggs.

Iodine is a component of thyroid hormones, which regulate metabolic rate.

Sources: Seaweed, saltwater fish, sea salt.

Selenium works with Vitamin E and is a cell membrane anti-oxidant.

    Sources: Broccoli, eggs, organ meat.

Cobalt is a part of Vitamin B12.

    Sources: Meat and shellfish.

Boron works with calcium and magnesium to build strong bones.

    Sources: Apples, nuts, pears, carrots.

Chromium (sometimes called Glucose Tolerance Factor) is needed to metabolize glucose.

    Sources: Brown rice, turkey, catnip.

Molybdenum is necessary for nitrogen metabolism.

    Sources: Liver, cereal grains, beans.

Silicon is necessary for collagen formation and maintenance of flexible arteries. It counteracts the toxic effects of aluminum. It helps heal wounds and wards off skin disorders.

    Sources: Beets, brown rice, bell peppers.

Doing It Right

*L*et's not forget one thing: we, as a species, long ago decided to domesticate these wild animals, these wolves and wild cats. We have taken them in because they worked, because they were useful, because they were a delight to have around. The deal now is, they can't feed like they used to. Our laws prohibit dogs from running down deer; in many places, laws prohibit pets from being outdoors without a leash. And in many municipalities, you don't want your cat stalking the neighborhood rats. Not any more. So *we* have to feed *them*. They can't feed themselves.

We owe it to these wonderful creatures to do the very best job we can—to give them food that will encourage happy, healthy lives. Sometimes it can be hard to keep a pet, harder still to feed them well. But think of your pet: hungry for nutrients, wanting to be full, wanting to feel secure in its feeding. Think of yourself, enjoying your pet's long and happy life with you. You've read this book; you've learned about what your pet needs and what you can do. You do have a lot of options, but in my view, feeding your pet indifferently, and in uninformed fashion, is not one of them.

Clearly, recent events surrounding the massive recall of pet food have given us all pause. Now it is time to act. I am not recommending that we abandon our huge commercial pet food industry, but I am saying that we can be part of an overall reform in how we feed our animals—a return, if you will, to the spirit of how animals used to be fed by their keepers. This will help pet food makers realize that indeed we do care enough about our pets to make the effort to feed them well. If we show the way, the industry will have to follow. It is up to us.

Good Product Sources

Commercial Pet Food

Flint River Ranch
www.frrco/7478
Makes high-quality dog and cat food and other products.

Nature's Logic
www.natureslogic.com
Also a good choice.

Neither of these brands, as of this writing, were involved in the pet food recall of 2007.

Supplements

Dynamite Marketing

www.dynamitemarketing.com

Vitamin supplements for pets, horses, birds.

Index

manufacturing of, 65, 66
myth about, 7
prescription, 83
preservatives in, 9
quality of, 26
vegetarian organic, 62
Dynamite Marketing, 150

eggs
    in cat recipes, 128, 130, 132
    in dog recipes, 118, 122
    importance of, 64
    raw, 64
    as source of vitamins and minerals,
        64
    as table scraps, 93
Eggs and Potatoes (dog recipe), 122–23
eggshell powder
    as calcium source, 121
    in cat recipes, 125, 126, 127, 129,
        132, 134
    in dog recipes, 119, 120, 121, 122,
        123, 124
    how to make, 121
entrée labels, 56
enzymes, 28, 88, 89, 109, 116, 126,
    131
ethoxyquin, 63, 68
Eukanuba, 27
extruders, 65–66

Fancy Feast, 27
fast food, 54
fasting, 38, 89
fat(s)
    animal, 62–63, 68
    AVMA recommendation about, 82
    and balanced diets, 48, 50
    benefits of, 12
    and cancer, 124
    and cat groupings, 112
    chicken, 68, 118, 122, 123, 131,
        132, 133
    in dog diets, 48
    and dog groupings, 101

in dog recipes, 115, 118
and history of pet food industry, 23
in homemade pet food, 48
importance of, 12
and labels on pet food, 57, 59,
    62–63, 68
and manufacturing of pet food, 65
myths about, 12
in pet food pie, 42, 44
poultry, 62–63, 123
preservation of, 63
sources of, 48, 50, 68
too much, 12
trans, 115
and vitamins, 137
fatty acids, 128, 137
feast-and-famine animals, 39
fiber, 49, 50, 77
fish
    in cat recipes, 126, 127, 129, 130,
        131, 132, 133
    and dog groupings, 106
    in dog recipes, 116, 119, 120
    and labels on pet food, 68
fish meal, 60, 65
Fish and Oats (dog recipe), 119
fish oil
    in cat recipes, 126, 127, 130, 133
    in dog recipes, 10, 116, 117, 119,
        122, 123
    helpful hints about, 133
    and homemade pet food, 81
    importance of, 12
flavorings, 77
flavors, on labels, 56
flaxseed oil, 85
Flint River Ranch, 92, 149
flours, and manufacturing of pet food,
    65
fluoride, 140
folic acid, 45, 136
Food and Drug Administration (FDA),
    19, 30, 31, 67
food groups, 48–50
For Feline Heart Care (recipe), 133

For Kidney Care I (cat recipe),
131–32
For Kidney Care II (cat recipe), 132
4 Ds (dead, diseased, dying and disabled
animals), 23
Friskies, 27
fruit
and balanced diets, 50
in cat diets, 43, 47
in cat recipes, 130
in dog diets, 43, 47
and dog groupings, 106
in homemade pet food, 81, 85
and pet food pie, 44
as snacks, 12
as table scraps, 77
See also specific recipe
fun facts
about cats, 100, 105, 110
about dogs, 100, 105
fungi, 64

Gaines, Clarence, 26
garlic, 74
Georgia (cocker spaniel), 2
ginger, 77, 143
gingerroot, 58
glucogenesis, 109
Glucose Tolerance Factor (chromium),
145
gluten meals, 61
grains
and balanced diets, 49
in canned pet food, 69
in cat diets, 43, 47
and cat groupings, 110
in cat recipes, 125, 126, 128, 129,
130, 134
in cereals, 76
in commercial pet food, 92
cooked, 90
in dog diets, 43, 47
and dog groupings, 102, 106, 107
in dog recipes, 116, 118, 119, 121
in dry food, 26, 61

and history of pet food industry, 23
in homemade pet food, 81, 84
and labels on pet food, 68
and manufacturing of pet food, 65
and pet food pie, 43–44
potential contaminants of, 65
protein in, 43–44
and raw food diets, 89, 90
sources of, 49
uncooked, 76, 84
See also specific recipe
grapes, 12, 50, 74, 80
grass, myth about, 22
Gravy Train, 27
grazing, 12
groupings
AKC, 101–4
for cats, 109–13
for dogs, 99–100, 101–7
Nation Way, 104–7
growth stimulants, 67

heart care
recipes for cat, 133
recipes for dog, 123
and vitamins, 136, 137, 138
heart rate, 105, 110
Heinz, 27
herbs, 77, 131, 143
herding dogs, 99, 101, 105, 106–7
Hill's Science Diet, 27
Holiday Dinner for Cats (recipe),
129
homemade pet food
AVMA recommendations about, 82,
83–84
and balanced diets, 47–48
cost of, 81–82
for dogs, 10–12, 47–48
ingredients in, 81
mixing table scraps and commercial
pet food with, 91–93
and need for change in pet food
industry, 19
pros and cons of, 79–85

origins, 60–61
See also cats; dogs
phosphorus, 45, 140
platter labels, 56
poodles, 2–3, 5, 102, 103, 104, 105
popcorn, 12
potassium, 45, 49, 140–41
potato chips, 12
potatoes, 76, 106, 107, 122–23, 127,
    134
Pottenger, Frances, 87–88
poultry
    AVMA recommendation about, 82
    by-products of, 60, 65
    in cat recipes, 126, 129
    and dog groupings, 106, 107
    in dog recipes, 116, 119, 120
    fat of, 62–63
    and labels on pet food, 62–63
    and manufacturing of pet food, 65
    in recipes, 115
    skin of, 73, 82, 84
    as table scrap, 73
    See also chicken
prescription dry food, 83
preservatives
    and acceptable commercial foods, 92
    in canned pet food, 9, 69
    and change in diets, 75
    in dry food, 9
    and labels on pet food, 56, 63, 68
    and manufacturing of pet food, 66
preventive medicine, 8
probiotics, 81, 115–16, 117, 126
Procter and Gamble (P&G), 27
protein
    and age of pet, 4
    animal, 59, 89, 102
    and balanced diets, 48, 49, 50
    in cat diets, 26, 42–43, 44, 47
    and cat groupings, 110
    in cat recipes, 125, 131
    in commercial pet food, 47
    in dog diets, 11, 43, 44, 47
    and dog groupings, 101–2

in dog recipes, 115, 122–23
and dry versus wet food, 7
and food groups, 48
and history of pet food industry,
    22–23
in homemade pet food, 47–48
and kidney disease recipes, 122–23,
    131
and labels on pet food, 57, 58, 59,
    61–62
and life stages, 57
and manufacturing of pet food, 65,
    66
and minerals, 144
myth about, 4
and origins and history of dogs, 37
in pet food pie, 42–44
quality of, 47, 48, 66
and raw food diets, 89
and rendering, 23, 24
sautéing of, 115
sources of, 11, 22–23, 43–44, 48,
    49, 50, 59, 61–62, 64, 75, 76, 89,
    101–2, 110
and variety in diets, 46
and vitamins, 136, 137
in wet food, 66
See also specific type of protein or recipe
Puppy Chow, 27
Purina, 27

quality
    and labels, 62
    of meats, 67
    of pet food, 51, 52, 62
    of protein, 47, 48, 66
    of wet food, 66

raisins, 12, 50, 74, 80
"ratters," terriers as, 103, 111
raw food
    in cat recipes, 134
    for cats, 87–88
    in homemade pet food, 84
    See also type of food